"For anyone who aspires to sit at the executive conference table, this book reveals the good, the bad, and the ugly that come with the job."

—*Jon Hanson, Vice President of Sales,*
*Cornerstone Software*

"*The Real Story of Informix Software and Phil White* provides very practical real-world business lessons intertwined with a rare view of a strong leader."

—*Adriaan Ligtenberg, Founder, Storm Technology,*
*C-Cube, and Takumi Technology*

"I found myself intrigued by the assertion that despite his personal failings, Phil White does not deserve the criminal treatment that the world seems all too eager to impose upon executives at the top of failed companies."

—*Angel Mehta,*
**The Sterling Report**

"Anyone who worked in the software industry during the heyday of the '90s will definitely enjoy this trip down memory lane."

—*Kapil Nanda, President and CEO,*
*Infogain*

"Informix was the dominant Silicon Valley story for many years. If you want to understand Silicon Valley, you have to study the rise and eventual consolidation of the database software industry."

—*Tom Foremski, Founder and Publisher,*
*Silicon Valley Watcher*

# THE REAL STORY *of* INFORMIX SOFTWARE *and* PHIL WHITE

## LESSONS IN BUSINESS
## AND LEADERSHIP
## FOR THE EXECUTIVE TEAM

**Steve W. Martin**

SAND HILL PUBLISHING
RANCHO SANTA MARGARITA, CALIFORNIA

Sand Hill Publishing
P.O. Box 80415
Rancho Santa Margarita, CA 92688

E-mail: info@storyofinformix.com
Web site: www.storyofinformix.com

**Ordering Information**
**Quantity sales.** Special discounts are available on quantity purchases by corporations, associations, and others. For details, contact the "Special Sales Department" at the address above.

**Individual sales.** Sand Hill publications are available through most bookstores. They can also be ordered directly from Sand Hill: www.storyofinformix.com.

**Orders for college textbook/course adoption use.** Please contact Sand Hill: www.storyofinformix.com.

**Orders by U.S. trade bookstores and wholesalers.** Please contact Biblio Distribution at 800-462-6420, F: 800-338-4550.

Martin, Steve W., 1960-
   The real story of Informix Software and Phil White / Steve W.
Martin.
    p. cm.
    Includes bibliographical references and index.
    ISBN 0-9721822-2-5
    1. White, Phillip E.  2. Informix Corporation.  3. Computer software industry—United States—History.  4. Entrepreneurship—California Santa Clara Valley (Santa Clara County).  5. High technology industries—California Santa Clara Valley (Santa Clara County)—History.  I. Title.
HD9696.65.U64 I54   2005
368.761—dc22              2005904034

Copyediting: PeopleSpeak
Cover Design: Catherine Lau Hunt
Interior Design & Production: Beverly Butterfield, Girl of the West Productions
FIRST EDITION
10  09  08  07  06  05     10 9 8 7 6 5 4 3 2 1

To Brooke, Michael,
and Emily,

This is the story of a once-great company where
your Dad worked from 1991 through 1997.

# Contents

# Preface

SILICON VALLEY HAS been around only for about sixty years, so it's still in its historical infancy. The history that has been written so far tends to romanticize the past, focus on the "geeks" who struck it rich, or relegate the Valley to trivia. For example, you probably have heard about David Packard's legendary Palo Alto garage, known as the "birthplace of Silicon Valley." Most certainly you have read about Larry Ellison, Steve Jobs, Jerry Yang, and the other high-tech billionaires. You may even know that the late Stanford University professor Fred Terman is the answer to the trivia question, "Who is the father of Silicon Valley?"

However, history is a collection of remembrances, and none of the existing writings accurately represent my Silicon Valley experience. I think this is due in part to the writers' motivation for recording the Valley's history in the first place. Some scribes have been zealous journalists in search of a career-making scoop. They sensationalized reality. Others were industry insiders who wrote to proliferate their ideas, expound their technology, or promote their company. They edited reality. And finally, some have been disenfranchised columnists who never worked for a high-technology company. Their purpose has been to denigrate the world's epicenter of wealth creation. They never truly experienced the reality of Silicon Valley.

My reasons for writing *The Real Story of Informix Software and Phil White* do not fall into any of these categories. First, I wrote this book to explain the incredible events surrounding the rise and fall of what was once a great company. Second, I wanted to record a unique chapter in Silicon Valley history between 1991 and 1997—the period after the technology recession of the late 1980s and before the Internet boom shifted into high gear in the latter half of the 1990s. Third, this book is a remembrance of a time when Silicon Valley mattered. We worked there with the hopes and dreams of making our marks on the world during a time frame that can be best described as California's second gold rush. While the environment was challenging and success was never guaranteed, back then we felt we had a fair chance of striking the "mother lode." We felt that we were taking part in history, not merely trying to survive and make a living like today. Finally and most importantly, history repeats itself. For the past five years, the Valley has experienced a malaise, and many of the business and sales strategies that enabled Informix to survive and succeed in similarly tough times and a hypercompetitive market are directly applicable today.

## INFORMIX SOFTWARE'S PLACE IN SILICON VALLEY HISTORY

History must be based upon the truth. While this book is primarily based upon my personal experience at Informix, I have incorporated public comments from company officials and customers and editorial comments from technology periodicals of the day to accurately reconstruct the times. You will also find private conversations with former employees along with quotations from relevant legal documents. Of primary importance are the in-depth interviews I held with Phil White, former Informix CEO (chief executive officer) on the eve of his imprisonment. From all of these sources, a picture of the truth emerges.

History does not usually make real sense until long after it has occurred. When I joined Informix Software in 1991, I had no idea of the tremendous highs and lows I would experience over the following six years. I witnessed a company grow from just over a hundred million dollars to a billion dollars in sales, from hundreds of employees to almost five thousand, and I saw a two-dollar stock rise, split, and increase to over ninety dollars. The times were exciting and the pace was frenetic. However, only through the passage of time have I been able to put these events into proper perspective.

In 1991, Informix was just one of many database suppliers in a market that included companies such as Sybase, Ingres, Unify, Progress, Interbase, and Empress. Together, we were competing against Oracle, the eight-hundred-pound Gorilla. In only four years, Informix was able to challenge Oracle's dominance, moving past all these other companies in the process. This was a truly remarkable feat and provides business lessons that are well worth studying today.

History records both triumphs and failures. History has a tendency to make some people feel good and others bad. Along with the accomplishments during my tenure at Informix, I also remember a company that launched products that no one wanted and that didn't work, squandered half a billion dollars on failed business strategies, and participated in a merger without winners. Worse yet, I witnessed Informix Software's complete collapse—culturally, ethically, and financially.

History is also full of surprises. Perhaps the biggest surprise happened when I viewed the following information on the Federal Bureau of Prisons Web site seven years after I left Informix.

| Inmate Information for PHILLIP E. WHITE | |
| --- | --- |
| Inmate Register Number: | 92769-011 |
| Name: | PHILLIP E. WHITE |
| Age: | 61 |
| Race: | WHITE |
| Sex: | MALE |
| Projected Release Date: | UNKNOWN |
| Location: | Lompoc |

This book details the history of Informix Software between 1991 and 1997. During this time, Phil White served as president, chairman, and CEO of the company. Throughout his tenure, Informix employees called Phil by his first name and he in turn called them by their last names. This naming convention has been kept throughout this book. In addition, the correct way to say the company name is "InFORmix," with the emphasis on the second syllable. Finally, the following timeline shows the chronology of major Informix-related milestones.

**Table 1.** Informix Timeline

| | |
|---|---|
| 1980 | Informix is founded by Roger Sippl as Relational Database Systems Inc. |
| 1986 | The company conducts an initial public offering and changes its name to Informix. |
| 1988 | Informix merges with Innovative Software and flounders financially. |
| 1989 | Phil White joins Informix as president and CEO. |
| 1991 | Oracle restates revenues and is hit with class-action lawsuits. |
| 1992 | Sybase is the darling of the database industry and is involved in a bitter war against Oracle. |
| | Informix voluntarily restates revenues for 1991. |
| 1993 | Oracle, Sybase, and Informix databases are on par technically. |
| | Informix stock is ranked number one for return on equity in the Silicon Valley Top 150. |
| | $32,000 worth of Informix stock purchased at 1991 low is now worth $1 million. |
| 1994 | Informix introduces an entirely rewritten database named OnLine Dynamic Server. |
| | Phil White is named *Financial World* magazine's CEO of the year for the second straight year. |
| | Enterprise application vendors, including PeopleSoft and SAP (Systems Analysis and Program Development), back Informix. |

1995    Sybase announces a first-quarter-revenue shortfall and is hit with class-action lawsuits.

Informix overtakes Sybase as the number one challenger to Oracle.

Informix stock is named the top five-year performer by the *Wall Street Journal*.

Informix purchases Illustra, an object-relational database software company, in December.

1996    Informix announces Universal Server, the merging of Informix and Illustra.

Phil White declares war on Oracle, sues the company, and calls it "sleazy."

Phil White receives NASDAQ's Legend in Leadership Award.

Informix posts $939 million in annual sales.

1997    Informix misses its first-quarter revenue projection, its first revenue miss in seven years.

Informix announces a $140 million loss for the first quarter, and class-action lawsuits are filed.

Phil White names Robert Finocchio Jr. president and CEO.

Phil White resigns as chairman. Informix restates revenues by $311 million for 1994–1996.

1998    Sybase restates revenues and is hit with class-action suits. Informix restates revenues for the second time in six months.

1999    Class-action lawsuits against Informix are settled for $142 million.

2000    Informix acquires Ardent Software for $880 million. Informix moves its operations from California to Ardent's Massachusetts headquarters.

2001    Informix database assets are sold to IBM for $1 billion.

2004    The Securities and Exchange Commission civil case against Phil White is settled.

Phil White pleads guilty to securities registration fraud in the criminal case. He serves a prison sentence at the United States Federal Correctional Institute at Lompoc, California.

# Introduction

*Whoever wishes to foresee the future must consult the past; for human events ever resemble those of preceding times. This arises from the fact that they are produced by men who ever have been, and ever shall be, animated by the same passions, and thus they necessarily have the same results.*

NICCOLO MACHIAVELLI

In 200 BC Emperor Shi Huangdi ordered the building of a great wall to keep the Mongols from attacking his empire. He dictated that the wall should be five men high and six horses wide, with watchtowers posted every three hundred feet. Surprisingly, invaders overcame this seemingly impenetrable barrier three times during the first one hundred years of its existence alone. The invading armies didn't have to take long marches around it nor incur huge losses trying to scale it in a massive frontal assault. All they had to do was bribe the guards who manned the gates. History tells us many important lessons if we choose to listen, like this one about strategy, tactics, and the eternalness of greed.

## THE PATRIARCH OF INFORMIX

In 1997 Phil White was the president, CEO, and chairman of Informix Software. But his importance went far beyond what these titles convey. He was the leader, visionary, guiding force, and patriarch of

Informix. In one sense, Informix and Phil White were one and the same. Even though the company had tens of thousands of shareholders and thousands of employees, Informix was his company.

He was also the greatest salesperson I have ever seen. This is a statement I do not make lightly since sales has been my profession for the past twenty years and I have written books on the subject. Whether Phil was communicating with employees, winning over the investment community, or persuading customers to buy, he spoke with a conviction and natural sense of ease that turned doubters into believers.

While many people described him as "charismatic," he possessed something greater. In my own terms he had "juice"—a presence that motivated others, instilled confidence, and gained their willing obedience. People sought his approval and would do almost anything to obtain it.

But working for Phil also had a contradictory and quirky side. Although a hands-off manager by nature, he wanted to be the center of control, and he personally named every Informix product. He was a technologist who could make sense of disjointed industrywide happenings, but he didn't use e-mail or computers and he wrote notes exclusively in longhand. He was also a somewhat aloof person. You felt you never really knew him personally, but you found yourself liking him just the same. While he had little empathy for nonperformers, he would be the first one to jump on a plane and fly anywhere in the world to help close a deal. Finally, he always left you with the impression that he was continually grading you into one of two columns: those who were helping the cause and those who weren't. Once a person was out of his good graces, his or her career at Informix was over.

Just as Phil engineered Informix's success, his single-minded obsession with Oracle and his desire to upstage its founder and CEO, Larry Ellison. eventually drove the company to ruin. Informix shocked its investors in the spring of 1997 when it reported an unexpected first-quarter loss of $140 million. Revenues were half those of the preceding quarter. As a result, Phil, the man who once said, "I don't think I have to fight Oracle,"[1] resigned as president and CEO on July 22, 1997. He was dismissed from the board of directors a week later when accounting irregularities were brought to the board's attention.

The Securities and Exchange Commission (SEC) subsequently began an investigation and ultimately concluded that Phil White signed financial statements knowing they were inaccurate. The SEC charged that Phil had inappropriately included revenue from contracts where side letters existed (secret agreements that enable customers to cancel contracts and receive their money back) and engaged in barter transactions with computer manufacturers where reciprocal purchases of hardware for software were made. At the SEC's urging, the Department of Justice began a criminal investigation that would go on for years.

## THE MOTHER OF ALL FINANCIAL ANNOUNCEMENTS

On November 18, 1997, Phil White's successor at Informix, former 3Com executive Robert Finocchio Jr. made the "the mother of all financial announcements": $311 million of revenues for the preceding three years had been overstated, and the company would restate revenues for 1994 through 1996.[2]

Informix's revenue restatement was by no means an isolated incident in the business world. The United States General Accounting Office reported that one of every ten publicly held companies restated their financial statements between 1997 and 2002 because of accounting irregularities that skewed financial results. As is usually the case, most of these restatements were lower than the original statements. In a total of 919 restatements, these companies lost an estimated $100 billion in market capitalization as a result.[3]

Furthermore, the Informix restatement was nowhere near the biggest in the high-technology industry. The information below taken from United States Securities and Exchange Commission databases shows a few of the recent restatements.[4]

Table 2. Recent Revenue Restatements of High-Technology Companies

| Restatement Years | Company | Amount (millions) |
| --- | --- | --- |
| 2001–2002 | Worldcom | $3,800 |
| 1995–2001 | Adelphia Communications | $2,300 |
| 2000–2001 | Qwest Communications | $2,200 |
| 2000–2001 | Computer Associates | $2,200 |
| 2000 | Lucent Technologies | $ 679 |
| 1999–2001 | Peregrine Systems | $ 509 |
| 1999–2002 | I2 Software | $ 359 |
| 1998–1999 | McKesson HBOC | $ 327 |
| 1994–1996 | Informix Software | $ 311 |

Revenue restatements are more than just accounting reversals. Their impact affects a company in every possible way. Customers are hesitant to purchase products, investors watch stock prices free-fall, employee morale is ruined (along with the value of employees' stock options), and flurries of class-action lawsuits are filed by lawyers eager to capitalize on misfortune. It's a devastating experience that almost always results in a management change and sometimes in bankruptcy. As I2's CEO and chairman said about the company's recent restatement, "Surely, the audit was no fun for us or our customers, and our customers were asked a lot of questions internally by their own people."[5]

If these restatements are "no fun," then why are they commonplace today? John Coffee Jr., professor of law at Columbia University, offers the following reasons: "First, there is intensifying or weakening of a particular company's stock, which usually occurs during a stock market bubble. Second, there is an overall decline in business morality and in the words of Federal Reserve Chairman an atmosphere of 'Infectious greed.' Third, the company has a weak board of directors who are not independent from senior management. Finally and most importantly, it's gatekeeper failure—the failure of the auditors, securities analysts, and securities attorneys, who prepare, review or analyze disclosure documents."[6]

When a restatement occurs, almost everyone loses, and Informix's auditor, Ernst & Young, was one of the biggest losers of Informix's 1997 restatement. In one of the largest securities fraud settlements in the history of Silicon Valley, Ernst & Young paid the majority of the cash portion of the $142 million required to settle the dozens of class-action lawsuits filed against Informix in 1999.[7]

While Professor Coffee would rightly argue that Informix's downfall was the result of greed, cronyism among the board of directors, and a gatekeeper that wasn't independent, I would like to suggest four additional reasons for revenue restatements that are specific to the high-technology industry.

- *Pride.* The high-tech industry is filled with leaders who have a fundamental desire to become rich and, equally important, famous. Since one of their most important possessions is their pride, they will go to any length to prove they are right and to avoid embarrassment, even if they have to cheat. I would argue that the CEOs' desire to protect their egos is just as powerful a motivator as greed.

- *Pressure.* The pressure starts at the local sales office, where proving oneself is a matter of survival. Pressure is exerted on the finance department to keep the numbers up. Pressure is on the gatekeeper to keep the client happy, and an incredible amount of pressure is placed on the CEO from investors, analysts, and the press alike. Pressure at all these points encourages revenue fraud.

- *Politics.* When the management regime changes at a troubled technology company, it is in the best interest of the new leaders to restate earnings and make the largest restatement possible. By doing so, they reset expectations extremely low and improve their likelihood of turnaround success. In other words, they debook as much revenue as possible, regardless of necessity, so that it can be recounted later and improve the financial numbers under their watch.

- *Past history.* History naturally repeats itself. Prior to Informix, Phil had served as the president of computer maker Wyse Technology. Wyse's CFO (chief financial officer), Howard Graham, would also become Informix's CFO. In 1989, Wyse Technology and company officials including White and Graham were sued for fraud and insider trading. According to court documents, computers were shipped "around the corner" to warehouses and then returned after the quarter ended. The lawsuit was settled in 1992 for $15.2 million in cash and served as a precursor of the future.[8]

## REVENUE RESTATEMENT LOSERS

While customers, investors, and employees all lose during a restatement, some of the biggest losers are usually the individuals who were responsible for the error (whether a mistake or fraud) in the first place. These executives are forced to disgorge themselves of their proceeds from stock sales for the period in question, assessed penalties and fines, prevented from serving as company officers in the future, and sometimes sentenced to prison. Let's examine typical punishments handed out to high-technology executives involved in revenue manipulations.[9]

The former CEO of one software company was convicted by a federal jury on charges of securities fraud. The evidence at trial established that he engaged in a scheme to overstate third-quarter revenues in 1999 by directing other employees to write side letters giving two customers a right to cancel their contracts and concealing those side letters from accounting personnel. Revenues from the two software sales transactions inflated sales by approximately $5 million. He was ordered to pay a $50,000 penalty and a $12,500 fine and serve twenty-seven months in prison.

The former president of another software and services company pled guilty to securities fraud in the third and fourth quarters of 2000. Specifically, he admitted his participation in six transactions that improperly recognized revenue. In one fraudulent transaction, he signed a side letter that gave a customer more time to pay for the software. In a transaction with a software company, he participated in negotiations for a quid pro quo exchange known as a "software swap." In this barter transaction, the companies exchanged software in order to inflate revenue numbers. He was sentenced to one year and one day in federal prison and ordered to pay a civil penalty of $110,000, a fine of $7,500, and restitution.

Many SEC investigations result in large fines and the return of monies made from stock sales. The copresident of one technology firm was ordered to return $733,360 and pay a civil penalty of $1 million. The CEO, COO (chief operating officer), and CFO of another software company were forced to disgorge approximately $10 million of stock proceeds and paid $350,000 each in fines.

Against this background, what happened to Phil White is quite surprising. Perhaps Phil's attorney spoke a little too soon when he said, "When Mr. White is ultimately cleared, we hope the public and the media will ask why an innocent man was forced to answer these baseless charges."[10] On May 12, 2004, Phil White pled guilty to one count of false statements in a registration statement, a felony.

Legal documents show that Phil White made $8,149,015 from the sale of Informix stock between February 7, 1995, and November 18, 1997.[11] However, the sentence judge Charles R. Breyer, brother of Supreme Court Justice Stephen Breyer, gave him was quite astonishing. The former *Financial World* magazine's CEO of the year for 1993 and 1994 was sentenced to a $10,000 fine, a $100 special assessment, and sixty days in prison.[12] It seems the world's greatest salesman had closed the biggest and best deal of his life.

Informix as a company was the ultimate restatement loser, and the times that followed were not particularly kind to the company. Following Phil's eight-year tenure, three CEOs would occupy the corner office in three years. After a less-than-successful merger with Ardent Software, the company was renamed "Ascential." In the bitter end, Informix's database assets were sold off to IBM in 2001 in what one analyst called "a fire sale, but nobody can find the fire."[13] As a database company, Informix no longer exists today. This is a sad statement about what was once a great company.

## CLOSING THOUGHTS

Nearly five hundred years ago William Shakespeare wrote one of his final tragedies. It's a play about a soldier who initially receives a hero's welcome upon his return from conquering the enemy. However, as the soldier tries to become a statesman, his pride infuriates the masses and he is sent into exile.

The story of Informix has all the essentials of a great Shakespearian tragedy. It's a story about the transformation of a laggard firm into one of the most respected companies in Silicon Valley. It's also the story of an overzealous press corps that was just as eager to promote the hero worship of the industry's high-tech leaders as it was to declare the same people as devils incarnate. It's also a story about a man who achieved the stardom he always craved and all the hometown recognition he always wanted but for all the wrong reasons. Finally, it's a story that continues to repeat itself at other high-tech companies around the world. And this shouldn't surprise anyone. History repeats itself because no one was paying attention the first time.

*The only thing new in the world is the history you don't know.*

HARRY S. TRUMAN

# 1

# Informix Background

## 1991 AND BEFORE

*If you would understand anything, observe its beginning and its development.*

ARISTOTLE

In order to understand the rise of Informix, it's necessary to understand a little about computers, how computers store information, and the evolution of software programming. In the late 1970s, the computers of the day all had something in common. Since the advent of the graphical user interface was still years in the future, all their screens were black with either a green or a yellow command line.

However, it was the differences between the various computers that made them frustrating. Each computer came with its own operating system and had its own commands and unique peculiarities. For example, the commands for an IBM mainframe were very different than for a Hewlett-Packard (HP) minicomputer. Working on a DEC VAX system was very different from working on an IBM PC with the disk operating system provided by a relatively unknown company called Microsoft.

Another major headache for programmers was that they couldn't run a completed program on a computer other than the one they wrote it on. Software written on a Digital Equipment computer wouldn't run on an IBM system and vice versa. Each of these computers was proprietary, meaning it ran only its own "flavor" of software. This

I

complete lack of interoperability was incredibly inefficient and limiting. Businesses and software manufacturers wanted their applications to be portable across the various vendors' computing platforms.

In the 1980s, the programming language most widely used within the business community was COBOL (common business-oriented language). Its popularity was due to its English-like commands. Prior to the advent of COBOL, programmers were mainly scientists who used cryptic, low-level languages to write applications. With COBOL, nonengineers could write and maintain software.

The data these COBOL programs accessed was usually stored in ISAM (indexed sequential access method) files. To access the data, programmers would write a series of calls in order to retrieve or write one record at a time. It was up to the programmers to ensure they were accessing the right data and that the records from different ISAM files were related. For example, an employee number from one file was associated with a name and an address in another.

At the end of the 1980s, a new technology movement started to gain momentum. The IT (information technology) community began storing information in new relational databases. Relational technology "managed" the relationships between the data for the programmers. However, these relational databases required more computer power to run because their processing overhead was greater than that of ISAM-based file systems. Now that faster, more powerful, and less expensive computers were available, relational technology became generally accepted and widely used.

## UNIX, RELATIONAL TECHNOLOGY, AND THE FUTURE

Like many executives within the software industry today, I began my career as a software programmer in the late 1970s. After working as a programmer for several years, I graduated to the position of system manager. Then my career made a most unexpected turn. The software company whose solution my company had implemented offered me a sales position. Selling software for this company over the next four years was great. Customers liked the functionality of our software and considered its underlying technology to be state-of-the-art.

However, a dramatic change was taking place in the marketplace in 1990. Our software ran only on HP 3000 minicomputers, and some companies were hesitant to buy it unless it ran on IBM, DEC, or Sun computers. Customers wanted the software to run on hardware they already had in place and knew how to operate. Others wanted independence from their existing hardware provider and the freedom to purchase the best product of the day (at the best price). However, it was impossible for us to port our solution to other platforms since it ran only on the MPE (multiprogramming executive) operating system and used HP's proprietary ISAM file system. It was partly because of these reasons that an obscure operating system called "UNIX" was gathering momentum in the marketplace.

What started out as a casual request in a very short time became a mandatory requirement. More and more companies were interested in the UNIX operating system. While UNIX was new to the business world, its promise of universal application portability across all computer manufacturers' hardware was extremely appealing. UNIX offered companies the freedom to select the best-in-class computers from any vendor. Never again would they be locked in to a single vendor.

Even worse for our company, Hewlett-Packard's sales organization seemed to jump on the UNIX bandwagon overnight. It wasn't interested in selling MPE-based systems anymore. It appeared that UNIX was the product of a coordinated strategy by all the hardware manufacturers to end IBM's domination of the industry at that point. UNIX, also known as "Open Systems," actually meant open competition against IBM. Suddenly, all the major hardware vendors, including Sun, HP, Digital, Silicon Graphics, NCR/AT&T, Sequent, Pyramid, Stratus, Unisys, Cray, Data General, and a very reluctant

IBM, were extolling the virtues of UNIX.

To add insult to injury, our biggest competitor had just completed an entire rewrite of its software onto Oracle's relational database. Now its software could run on any UNIX hardware platform, and it had superior relational technology compared to our ISAM-based solution. It seemed that the computing landscape had changed overnight.

Salespeople are the first sensors of market changes since they have the direct pulse of customers and their shifting buying habits. As information about this change in the industry was coming in from salespeople in the field, the leader of my company disputed and denied it. As evidence continued to accumulate, he retreated into his office to create spreadsheet scenarios that could never be attained.

Faith and hope are perhaps two of the greatest assets of any technology company. When they vanish, employees leave, customers refuse to buy products, and in the long term the company is doomed. Even though I had been with this company for several years and my coworkers were some of my closest friends, my faith in its leader was lost and my hope that the company would somehow find a way to succeed was destroyed.

Given these circumstances, I had only one option: find a new job—specifically, a sales job with a company that focused on UNIX and supported relational technology. After contacting the vice president of sales of half a dozen companies, I received a response from a company called "Informix." Informix was an abbreviation for Information UNIX. The company focused on providing relational database technology for the UNIX operating system. It seemed like the right move, and I was hired as one of the company's first salespeople in Southern California. My first day on the job would be at the annual sales kickoff.

## INFORMIX SALES KICKOFF, 1991

It was common practice for technology companies to hire as many salespeople as possible prior to an annual sales kickoff, the sales meeting at the beginning of each year where the company vision is presented, new marketing programs are launched, and product features and functionality are reviewed. It's one of the best ways to get new hires up to speed, acclimate them to the company's culture, and acquaint them with their new teammates.

The 1991 Informix sales kickoff was held in Scottsdale, Arizona. The sales organization would spend three days in the main ballroom listening to presentations. The audience was predominantly white males ranging in age from their late twenties to early forties. Being a former athlete seemed to be a key hiring criterion because all the salespeople looked like they had played sports in the past.

In hindsight, this shouldn't have been surprising. The first lesson learned that first day was that selling for Informix was not easy. The competition was intense, and Oracle and Sybase were far ahead of Informix in both name recognition and technology. Losing deals to both of them was commonplace. Although it may sound strange, people who have played sports actually know how to lose. They are able to handle emotional disappointments, bounce back from a loss, and get themselves ready for the next game. After losing, they don't shy away from stiff competition and big challenges but instead continually seek other opportunities to redeem themselves.

Another lesson learned that day was that the lives of the Informix salespeople revolved around their jobs, not the other way around. In this way, too, selling for Informix was like playing a sport. The long hours required of an athlete, whether on a baseball diamond, on a football field, on a tennis court, or in a swimming pool, paralleled the schedule of a successful Informix salesperson. Most importantly, sports teach how to take advantage of an opponent's weaknesses and to execute countermoves to win. All of these attributes inherent in playing sports were directly applicable to becoming a successful Informix salesperson.

Early on the first day of the 1991 sales kickoff, everyone found a seat and made idle chitchat while the emcee reviewed the day's agenda. Then he introduced the headline speaker, Phil White. A perceptible change in the atmosphere took place. All talking stopped, people sat more upright, and some took out notepads. It was quite obvious that the person everyone called "Phil" was in total control of the room.

In his presentation, Phil talked about the future of UNIX and how client-server applications would become commonplace because users demanded access to mainframe data. He lectured about how companies sought vendor independence and why UNIX was the only operating system that could provide this freedom. With a self-assured demeanor, he reviewed Informix's financial position. Even though some members of the audience may have been confused by the complex financial topics he spoke of, he appeared to know exactly what he was talking about. He presented Informix's future technology plans and gave the impression he had his finger on the pulse of the industry. He spoke with congruence and a conviction that went beyond spoken words. In other words, I absolutely believed that he believed in what he was saying. The audience seemed to be thankful that he was the leader in charge.

Sales kickoffs always include a lot of mandatory team-building events, and the following day everyone was required to meet by the pool in swimsuits. I happened to be sitting in the Jacuzzi prior to the team competitions when a nondescript fellow sat down next to me. Because of his look, his demeanor, and the fact he was wearing a Speedo, my first thought was that he was a technical type or perhaps a foreigner. We made small talk for a few minutes, then I formally introduced myself and asked what he did for Informix. He gave me kind of an incredulous look and said, "I'm Roger Sippl, the founder and chairman of the company." Then he got up and left. I couldn't believe my faux pas and hoped he wouldn't remember my name.

## THE ODD COUPLE: ROGER SIPPL AND PHIL WHITE

Roger Sippl and Phil White were different in many ways. While Phil was dashing and debonair and had the natural good looks that complemented his role of CEO, Sippl was much more introverted and looked more like an accountant. The paths that led each to Informix were very different. Sippl lived in the Bay Area and had studied computer science at the University of California, Berkeley. He was an entrepreneur-technologist. Phil grew up in the Midwest and had spent sixteen years at IBM. He was a man on a mission to reach the top of the corporate ladder.

Sippl graduated from Berkeley in 1977 with a bachelor of science degree. Berkeley was considered a big "UNIX school," and Sippl would later say this of his college days: "As students we were using UNIX version 6. That was the hot, exciting computer to be taught on; the other students had to use batch processing machines with punch cards, but if you were really lucky you got into the classes and got to be taught computer science on the interactive UNIX systems."[1]

After graduation, Sippl set out to find a job but soon found that his UNIX experience didn't help him. "I was quite disappointed that none of the job ads in the classified section said anything about UNIX. They all wanted all sorts of initials that I'd never heard of in Berkeley—DOS, VSC, CICS, OS, all these different mainframe operating systems I was completely unfamiliar with."[2] One of his interviews was with Steve Jobs at Apple. Since he didn't know how to program 6502 assembly language, he didn't get the job. The suit and tie he wore to the interview probably didn't help win over the countercultural Jobs either.

Sippl went on to perform consulting work at Bechtel on its high-end million dollar minicomputers and at Cromemco, a business-oriented microcomputer company. "I was making a lot of money as a consultant, but I wanted to get out of the mode of an hour worked, a dollar earned. The notion of taking a thousand hours of effort and producing a piece of packaged software as many times as you can appealed to me."[3]

Three years after graduating from Berkeley, Sippl started Relational Database Systems with a fellow programmer from Bechtel and Cromemco. "I was watching the packaged software business on microcomputers. The price points were remarkably different—a few hundred dollars for a product on a microcomputer versus a few hundred thousand dollars for a product on a mainframe—there wasn't much of a packaged software market for minicomputers."[4]

An unwritten formula in high technology goes something like this:

Entrepreneur + Technology Foresight + Silicon Valley = Success

Roger Sippl provided the first two parts of this equation when he started Relational Database Systems. His company would focus on the business market and create database management software for minicomputers instead of mainframes. He recruited high school and college friends to get the business off the ground, and by 1985 the company had nearly one hundred employees. The following year the company went public and changed its name to Informix.

The Valley is filled with many "one-hit wonders," entrepreneurs who were able to take one company from an idea to a successful IPO (initial public offering). Sippl is one of the few serial entrepreneurs who has hit several home runs in his career with Informix, with customer-relationship software provider Vantive, and with object request broker software company Visigenic. In comparison to Sippl, Phil White had a quite different background.

## SMALL-TOWN BOY MAKES GOOD

A native of Pana, Illinois, Phil White grew up near the geographical center of the state. A small town of five thousand, Pana is one of the fifteen towns and cities that make up Christian County. According to the 2000 census, 99.6 percent of the town's residents were white and 88.7 percent were born in Illinois. Far from the affluence of Silicon Valley, in 1999 the median household income was $29,611, the average mortgage payment was $613, and only five families had an income greater than $150,000.[5]

Even as a boy, Phil was known to be enterprising. He mowed lawns, shined shoes, and worked at the local golf course as a caddy. He was a prodigious saver, and the highlight of his week was going to the bank on Saturday morning to make his weekly deposit. He made so many deposits that his savings book frequently filled, much to the chagrin of the local bank tellers.

On the surface, this son of an accountant and a teacher seemed to live an "Ozzie and Harriet" type of childhood. To some extent he did. He was a Boy Scout who won awards for carving figurines and wooden neckerchief slides. In high school, he was a multisport athlete and a thespian. However, his father was an ardent gambler who owned a pool hall. The card games that were held in its back room were the scuttlebutt of the town, even though the mayor and many of the town's prominent citizens played in them.

A 1961 graduate of Pana High School, Phil returned in 1997 to deliver the commencement address and be enshrined on the Pana High School Wall of Fame.

Throughout his college years and after his graduation, Phil worked as a tour guide. He would take a couple of hundred people to the Rose Bowl, New Orleans, or Hawaii. However, he soon realized the owner's son would inevitably take over the company. He later said of his decision to leave the tour business, "I didn't want to just work, I wanted to run the thing. I didn't go to school to be second fiddle."[6]

One of his tour guide friends encouraged him to interview with IBM. After joining the company as a salesman, he steadily climbed the IBM corporate ladder. In order to get ahead, he made frequent strategic job moves and relocated six times over the next sixteen years. When faced with the decision between moving to Japan in order to reach the next rung on the ladder or leaving IBM for a job in Silicon Valley, he chose to move out west.

Phil joined Altos Computer Systems in San Jose as senior marketing vice president in 1984. In this role, Phil was charged with a task he was well suited for and loved to do—spearheading the drive to win major OEM (original equipment manufacturer) customers. In OEM sales, one company buys another's technology and embeds it within its products. These deals are very different from ordinary sales to end customers. These strategic agreements are discussed and negotiated at the highest levels within companies. Sometimes they result in complex partnerships where one company invests in the other. Most importantly for technology companies, these large deals escalate revenue exponentially, provide an immediate infusion of cash, and instantly expand the customer base.

One of Altos Computer's key OEMs was Wyse Technology, a leading manufacturer of dumb computer terminals that was second only to IBM in market share. In just five years, Wyse had grown from $200,000 in sales to more than $125 million. Altos owned 26 percent of Wyse and held a seat on its board of directors, a seat that Phil occupied.

When Wyse began actively seeking a president and CEO, Phil and Wyse cofounder Bernard Tse came to the agreement that Phil was the best candidate for the job. According to Tse, "One day after a board meeting, Phil and I were standing in front of the building. We thought about Phil at about the same time he thought about

Wyse."[7] After two years at Altos, Phil left to become the president and COO of Wyse Technology.

Phil's decision to leave Altos was a complete surprise to Altos chairman Dave Jackson. "They've got a good man," he said. "What they need I suppose quite badly are OEM accounts and a sense of direction, and he'll supply those."[8] Phil said, "The hardest thing about this was leaving Altos. There was absolutely nothing wrong there. Dave Jackson and I are very close. There's no animosity or bad feelings. The Valley's pretty small. Once you decide to do something, you should go ahead and do it and get it over with."[9] In many ways, these words echoed Phil's philosophy of putting business ambition over personal friendships and action over indecision.

Wyse was planning an ambitious move into the desktop computer market. However, the company shipped systems with a plethora of technical defects: they overheated and occasionally caught fire, the hard drives would randomly erase data, and the circuit boards were faulty. When the company missed its predicted revenue targets in 1988, a class-action lawsuit was filed on behalf of disappointed shareholders. The suit alleged that Phil had inflated revenues by fraudulently shipping systems that hadn't been ordered. In addition, they argued he misled investors when he said they would hit their quarterly revenue target when in fact they missed it. The case was settled prior to going to trial for $15.2 million.[10] The board of directors had decided to sell the company and knew it would not attract serious offers with the lawsuit pending.

While in the process of selling Wyse, Phil received a phone call from an executive recruiter about the search for a new leader at Informix Software. Since he knew Sippl from his days at Altos, he had the inside track for the job as president and CEO, and he joined Informix in January of 1989. His main task at hand would be to unite a company that was equally divided between Silicon Valley and Lenexa, Kansas.

## WHERE IS LENEXA, KANSAS?

Each night during the 1991 sales kickoff there were group dinners and partying till early morning. The drinking was of epic proportions. During these parties, employees would eagerly voice their opinions, bestow their advice, and volunteer all sorts of secrets to newcomers such as me.

Three basic groups of people were at the Scottsdale sales kickoff: salespeople from all around the world; technical and marketing staff from headquarters in Menlo Park, California; and staff from Lenexa, Kansas. Somehow, the folks from Lenexa didn't fit in. They didn't mix with the others but instead milled mainly among themselves. This left the impression that they weren't genuinely welcomed at the event but tolerated instead. They were like distant cousins who had been invited to the family Christmas party. People were polite to them but thankful they wouldn't see them again till next year.

The Lenexa attendees were the result of Informix's disastrous merger with desktop automation publisher Innovative Software in 1988. While the merger made Informix the tenth largest publicly owned packaged software company at the time, it was also the catalyst that brought Phil to Informix. The merger had been far more difficult than expected. Sales and marketing costs skyrocketed, product development was in disarray, and no one knew who was really running the company, California or Kansas.

Innovative was the publisher of desktop automation software products Smartware and Wingz. Smartware was an all-in-one word processor, spreadsheet, and database for DOS. Wingz was a state-of-the-art graphical spreadsheet that could access back-end databases via structured query language calls. Informix had high hopes that the merger would provide the company with end-to-end products from the front-end desktop to the back-end database. As Roger Sippl explained, "The merging of the database world and the office automation world is, I think, long overdue. It's always a mystery to me how those worlds got so separate and stayed apart for so long."[11] Ideally, Innovative's retail channel sales strategy would enhance Informix's direct sales strategy. However, this sales dichotomy created far more problems than opportunities in reality.

Unfortunately, Innovative's flagship product, Smartware, was past its prime, and a subsequent release to match Microsoft's and Lotus's product capabilities was more than a year late. Ironically, the sexy 3-D graphical Wingz spreadsheet that so much hope was pinned on was available only on Macintosh systems. Since Windows had become the corporate standard, Wingz was moot from the start. When a port for Windows was finally released more than a year behind schedule, the graphical capabilities of Excel matched those of Wingz. As one senior sales executive lamented over a cocktail at the sales kickoff, "Nothing good ever comes out of Lenexa."

The merger was a complete clash of cultures and a source of friction as executives from both organizations served their different agendas. As a result, two separate companies were running under the Informix name, a technology-driven UNIX company in Silicon Valley and a PC-focused retail publisher in the farm belt. One former Informix vice president said, "There was a big rift between Lenexa and Menlo Park. You had people in Lenexa who thought the people in Menlo Park were strange because they were Californians. And there were people in California who thought the people in Kansas were country bumpkins."[12] Informix was in chaos and the bottom line was impacted. While sales grew 51 percent in 1988, profit fell 84 percent to its lowest mark in four years. The company also announced a loss for the fourth quarter of $2.6 million.[13]

Phil tried to frame the merger in the best possible light when he said, "Good move, poorly executed, but working out."[14] But no matter how it was spun, the merger cost the company much pain, money, and embarrassment. An article by Joshua Greenbaum in *Software Magazine* said of the merger, "Not only did Informix buy a spreadsheet that couldn't compete against Excel and Lotus 1-2-3, but it tried to do a 'friendly' merger with Wingz parent company, based in Kansas. This resulted in a shuttle diplomacy between Informix HQ and the heartland that would have even taxed Henry Kissinger. By the time the hayseed had settled, Informix's stock was in the toilet, its management in disarray, the lawyers were circling like vultures, and its customers and partners were nervous."[15] Phil was brought in to take action and fix the merger mess.

## REGROUP AND REATTACK

It was a critical time for Informix because the company had lost momentum because of the merger. Roger Sippl said, "1989 will be the year we find out what we are really made of; we have the opportunity to regroup and re-attack."[16] The reattack began as soon as Phil White joined the company. On his second day on the job as president, he cut 15 percent of the company's employees. The majority were from Lenexa or associated with the desktop products.

More importantly, he reorganized operations, clearly placing Menlo Park in control. According to one former Informix vice president who was quoted at the time, "The company needed someone to stand up and say, 'Hey, follow me.' And, Roger wasn't that guy."[17] Phil took charge immediately, and within ninety days the company's financial picture improved significantly. "In my first 90 days we went from a 21-cent loss to a 4-cent profit. It's not the amount of profit that we made, but the turnaround," Phil boasted to the local press.[18]

Phil was unafraid to make difficult and unpopular decisions. He stopped all development and support of a version of the Informix database for DEC's VMS proprietary operating system. This was a highly charged decision within Informix and for customers who had previously bought the product. One VMS customer said, "Unfortunately we only found out a couple of months ago that Informix announced the death of Informix for VMS. This is even despite us being a maintenance customer. Naturally, I and all the computing professionals around here have now sworn off Informix and its total product line for life!"[19]

The die was now cast. Informix was solely a database company, and the company went back to its UNIX roots. It would focus only on products that helped sell databases. An industry analyst from the investment advisor firm Hambrecht & Quist said, "White has refocused Informix and instilled the sense that Informix is a database company that sells office automation tools, not the other way around."[20] Informix had found its focus again.

However, the Innovative episode had one unexpected casualty. Since Informix was first and foremost a UNIX database company, any interest in the client's desktop disappeared. The software that was running on the desktop became a secondary concern. In one sense this was great because UNIX as a back-end platform was growing faster than any other. In another way, it was an ominous sign of the future. Informix would never release a truly successful product for Microsoft Windows or Microsoft NT. Porting software to these platforms was an afterthought. Informix considered it more of a necessary evil, unlike Oracle and Sybase, which saw it as a true business opportunity.

The UNIX mind-set within Informix was pervasive. At corporate headquarters you would see more UNIX workstations running Openlook or Motif graphical user interfaces than personal computers running Windows. Early on, salespeople were even taught how to use the UNIX-based Eudora e-mail program and expected to learn Vi, the unfriendly, awkward UNIX line command word processor (instead of Microsoft Word). While the 1991 sales kickoff provided a crash course on the company's history and challenges, no one bothered to mention practical information like this to the newcomers on the sales staff.

## WHAT THEY DON'T TELL YOU CAN KILL YOU

Another taboo topic at the sales kickoff was that several of the company's senior executives were dating within the company. Phil's first wife had been a secretary whom he had met while working at IBM. When their marriage ended in 1990, Phil began dating Cindie Lozano, who worked in the Informix marketing department, and he would eventually marry her. She left the company shortly after their relationship became serious. Interoffice dating was considered a normal part of the Silicon Valley culture at the time and at Informix in particular. Numerous senior executives would date and go on to marry coworkers. However, it was important to keep track of who was dating whom. You surely didn't want to offend the girlfriend of one of the senior staff members.

The sales kickoff produced another interesting revelation—that in one sense, the sales organization was an amalgamation of cliques. North American sales comprised four regions: eastern, midwestern, southern, and western. There was more than a friendly rivalry between the various regions. Each region was on a mission to prove it was the best. Although all the salespeople were intensely competitive individuals by nature, they also supported and rooted for their regional teammates.

Meanwhile, the North American team competed against the teams representing EMEA (Europe, Middle East, and Africa), Latin America, and Asia Pacific areas. As in most other software companies, over half of Informix's revenue typically came from North America. However, the proportion of international sales was rising—from 39 percent in 1988 to 45 percent in 1990.[21]

The resulting peer pressure inside the sales organization was tremendous. If you didn't achieve your quarterly revenue targets, not only did you fail personally, but you let your region down. You didn't help defeat the other worldwide sales areas. On the other side of the coin, when you posted a great quarter, you were honored and respected by your team. This "sales culture" was very different from the individualistic "every man for himself" culture of the hired guns at Oracle. Informix fostered a team environment.

Informix was a collection of individuals trying to succeed as a team. One senior salesperson described Informix as a bunch of ants who worked with their heads down as fast and hard as possible on their part of the anthill, not knowing what anyone else was doing. Once a year, the ants all got together at a sales kickoff to take a look at how the hill was coming along.

However, the competition between North American sales and European sales was more than a rivalry; it was an ongoing war. Each organization and its leaders were out to prove themselves better than the other. The prevalent thinking throughout the sales organization was that the vice president who decisively won the battle would go on to become the head of worldwide sales. However, Phil never had any intentions of promoting either leader into this coveted position. Rather, he encouraged the rivalry as it brought out the best in both teams.

Even with all the contention, conflict, and drama within the sales force, everyone was united in the common cause of defeating Oracle and Sybase. While Oracle was disliked, picking a fight with a company six times the size of Informix wasn't necessarily a prudent decision. Sybase, on the other hand, was a different story. It was about Informix's size but growing faster. Sybase was winning all the blue-chip accounts and making it look easy in the process. Meanwhile, we had to scramble to make our number from quarter to quarter. We called ourselves "dirt farmers" because we had to somehow make our number from scratch every quarter.

The desire to defeat Sybase unified the sales force around a single cause. Sybase was truly despised, the focal point of Informix's anger. The anonymous Middle Eastern saying "Me against my brother, my brother and I against the world" expresses the way the sales force was a band of brothers committed to destroying Sybase.

As the 1991 Scottsdale sales kickoff ended, everyone was anxious to get back to the office and start selling. We were pumped up after three days of Informix propaganda and partying. However, my first disappointment came shortly after returning home. The manager who had hired me announced he was leaving the company. During my first year I would report to four different sales managers, each from a different part of the region. As difficult as that was, it was nothing compared to what lay ahead for me on sales calls.

## AN UNFAIR FIGHT IN LARGE ACCOUNTS

Selling for Informix was grueling hand-to-hand combat. We were outnumbered by Oracle, our technical weaponry was inferior to Sybase's, and we were not as well-known as Ingres. When we went on sales calls, we developed the habit of casually thumbing through the visitors log at the reception desk. What we saw was almost always the same, and it was very discouraging. When Oracle made a sales call, it would typically "unload the bus." This sales strategy term made famous by IBM involves bringing in as many people as possible on a sales call to show a company's depth, breadth, and market dominance.

In addition to the local salesperson and sales manager, Oracle would bring database presales engineers, application development tools engineers, experts from its business accounting applications, industry marketing specialists from whichever vertical the prospect was a part of (manufacturing, retail, consumer packaged goods, government, and so on), and consultants who would help implement the software. It was impressive, and the bigger companies that were used to dealing with IBM responded positively as expected.

Not only were we outnumbered ten to one by Oracle's salespeople, but they were invited into every account while we had to pry the customer's door open. We had to prove to these big companies that it was worth their time and effort to even meet with us. Meanwhile,

Oracle was the eight-hundred-pound gorilla that did whatever it pleased. After working hard on one Fortune 500 account, we were finally granted permission to make a presentation to its evaluation team. A day before the presentation, the customer called and canceled. We later learned that Oracle had threatened to drop out of the deal if the customer was still looking at beginner products like Informix's. It's hard to imagine one company having that kind of power—but it did!

Since the Internet was not as pervasive then as it is today, customers had four basic ways to get information: from the vendors themselves; through industry periodicals and publications such as *Computerworld, InformationWeek,* and *DBMS Magazine;* from industry analyst firms like the Gartner Group and AMR Research; and perhaps most importantly, from newsgroups and electronic bulletin boards where respective users shared their opinions and personal experiences with vendors' products.

These newsgroups and bulletin boards were the precursors of the Internet chat rooms, customer opinion Web sites, and blogs (web logs) people use today to find unedited information. Through these forums, database administrators held technical discussions, had heated philosophical debates, and shared the daily news about the industry. They played a powerful role in influencing customers' perceptions and buying habits. Here's an example of a common topic of conversation—Oracle's high-pressure sales tactics back in 1991: "An Oracle representative told me that unless we generate at least $50,000 of revenue per year and we spent at least $5,000 per year for support, training and development tools, they are not interested in doing business with us. Before you order any Oracle product, ask Oracle if they are still interested to have you as a customer after you tell them how much you plan to spend."[22]

Meanwhile, at Informix we were excited about a $50,000 order since our average order was around $20,000. With very few exceptions, we were relegated to minor purchases made for departmental applications. We weren't selected to be the strategic infrastructure platform like Oracle. Customers bought our products because they were easy to install and maintain and a lot of third-party applications were built on Informix. We were also priced competitively, 15–20 percent below Oracle and Sybase.

Oracle wanted complete control of all of a customer's technology investments. It wanted the biggest customers to use its application development tools and database and to deploy its business applications (accounting, inventory, manufacturing, etc.). It wanted to supply customers with consulting services to implement these products. Oracle sold end-to-end business solutions. Meanwhile, we were the UNIX database guys and, quite frankly, we were out of Oracle's league.

Sybase presented an entirely different set of challenges. Sybase was the darling of the industry, and the analyst community loved the company. These analysts were in a much more powerful position over the technology vendors than today's analysts. The most important analyst was the Gartner Group. Its regularly published "Magic Quadrant," a graph that showed how the vendors compared against each other, was one of the key influencers of customer buying behavior.

The Magic Quadrant is a square divided into four equal-size smaller squares. Every vendor's goal was to be as close to the top and far to the right in the top right-hand "leader" square as possible. The leaders were vendors who were performing well at the time, had a clear vision of market direction, and were actively building competencies to sustain their leadership position in the market. Sybase was consistently ranked as the leader, even above Oracle, while Informix vacillated between the bottom quadrants.

Industry publications also proclaimed Sybase's technical superiority, which in fact was true at that time. Sybase had three key technical features that Oracle and Informix didn't offer: stored procedures, triggers, and two-phase commit. Stored procedures let database administrators place frequently used operations within the database instead of populating them individually across all the client's personal computers. A trigger is an event that automatically fires a stored procedure or another action. For example, when the value of a certain field drops below a predefined threshold, the software triggers an event, such as a report or an e-mail. Two-phase commit ensures that disparate databases remain synchronized when a transaction updates multiple databases; either all or none are updated.

What made these features so appealing to customers and damaging to other vendors was the way Sybase's salespeople explained them. Sybase was very popular with Wall Street investment firms, a fact the company still touts to this day. The Sybase salespeople would say something like, "Do you know why the majority of the securities companies on Wall Street, including Goldman Sachs, Smith Barney, and Fidelity Investments, use Sybase? Because we never lose a transaction. Now I'm sure you don't want to lose any transactions either, and we have the only DBMS that can guarantee this because of our support of two-phase commit. We are the only DBMS that provides advanced features to ensure the best business decisions are made. For example, stored procedures and triggers help ensure trades occur automatically under the ideal conditions when predetermined thresholds are encountered." By presenting their arguments in this manner, the salespeople ensured that the clients concluded their product was technically superior and better suited for mission-critical environments. Meanwhile, we had to go to great lengths trying to prove ours was just as capable.

Although Ingres had been around longer than Sybase and Informix, the company had floundered for years. In a *UnixWorld* magazine article, noted industry analyst Rich Finkelstein said, "Its marketing is not up to par. Ingres has good technology, but it's a secret." Facing a financial crisis, Ingres was acquired by Ask Computer Systems, a provider of manufacturing applications, in 1990. Once the acquisition occurred, customers lost interest in evaluating the company's products. Its stature in the marketplace diminished further as its product development and marketing budgets were continually slashed. Finkelstein commented further, "The company has no clear message as far as what it wants to achieve—that got gumbled up with the ASK acquisition."[23] In 1994 Ingres was sold again to Computer Associates, and the best days of the products were in the past.

Here's how one newsgroup user summed up Oracle, Sybase, Ingres, and Informix at the time (1991).

> Oracle: "Shark" attitude (milk you for all they can get).
> Huge user base.
> Sybase: Seem to have the top rated product.
> Ingres: Seems to have one of the best products, technically.
> Informix: Good product, but lacking in several features.[24]

The size of Oracle's user base was a huge competitive advantage. It gave managers of information technology departments proof they were buying a product that would be around for the long term. It gave database administrators something even more powerful: a sense of comfort because they were learning a marketable skill. Database administrators had two golden rules about buying software. No product, however good it is, is worth buying if the company dies, and no product, no matter how bad it is, is that bad if it helps you get your next job. This second golden rule also applied to other decision makers, ranging from programmers to CIOs, across all sizes of companies.

## COMPETING IN SMALL AND MID-SIZED COMPANIES

For Informix salespeople, competing for sales to smaller companies was in some ways even worse than competing for big accounts. Smaller companies took the exact opposite approach of big companies and invited everyone to make presentations, including Oracle, Sybase, Ingres, Informix, Unify, Progress, Interbase, Empress, and sometimes Foxpro. While it was exciting for us to get an inbound phone call once in a while, the thrill would be short-lived.

Time and time again, Informix wouldn't win these deals either, and a pattern of customer behavior became clear. It seemed that very early in the sales cycle, most likely even before all the vendors were contacted, the customers had already made up their minds on which product to buy.

One vendor always had an unfair advantage, going into the formal evaluation process as the default decision. Dethroning the chosen vendor then was an extremely tough task since the company had an opportunity to build a personal relationship with the customer beforehand. Because a decision had already been made, all the other vendors would jump through the customer's sales process hoops and present, benchmark, and install evaluation software for nothing.

However, the customers also had a dilemma. They still wanted to collect information from the other vendors to be 100 percent certain they were selecting the right database. At times, the selection of a database was a highly charged political issue. Therefore, the decision makers wanted to complete the evaluation process to show others within or outside their organization (management, colleagues, consultants, or government agencies) that their evaluation was thorough and fair. As a result, many customers would say anything to keep other vendors in the evaluation.

For a vendor, this is a strange predicament to be in. The customers know they aren't going to choose your solution, but they can't tell you that you won't win. Therefore, they tell you what they think you want to hear.

Customers would give us false signs that they were more interested in buying our product than they actually were. For example, the first question a customer asked might be, "Do you have stored procedures, triggers, and two-phase commit?" When we answered no and asked them if these features were important, they would say, "Not really," when in fact they used the lack of these features as justification to eliminate Informix in their minds.

Conversely, customers wouldn't share critical information or access to other people in the company with us as they did with their favorite database company. Oracle enjoyed frequent meetings with the CIO (chief information officer) and CTO (chief technology officer). We were relegated to talking with database analysts and engineers. Unfortunately, we would continue to spend additional resources and time on an account when a decision for Oracle had been made already at higher levels.

We learned a valuable lesson from all this losing: whether inadvertently or on purpose, the customer always lied. One of an Informix salesperson's primary responsibilities was to determine whether a customer was lying and whether we had an honest opportunity to win the deal.

We learned another important lesson. If we were not in the deal from the very beginning, we would most likely lose because we didn't have a relationship with the customer. Therefore, even though we were battling Oracle and Sybase on a daily basis, our real enemy was time. We wasted it working on deals where we didn't belong in the first place.

## CHOOSING THE RIGHT BATTLES TO FIGHT

Picking the right battles to fight was the secret to sales success at Informix. We could never go toe to toe against Oracle. We couldn't make a frontal assault based upon technical functionality against Sybase. We were spinning our wheels when we came late into a deal because the customers most likely had already made up their minds. But we saw four places where we could win: applications, hardware partners, UNIX zealots, and education of the outcasts and ignored.

- *Applications.* Several hundred independent software companies had built their applications using Informix's database and tools. In general, these solutions were not the popular enterprise software solutions available at the time from Dun and Bradstreet and JD Edwards. The independent software companies were niche players that had developed applications for specific verticals such as hotel property management, higher education accounting, or legal office automation. Since they usually didn't have large sales forces, we became their eyes, ears, and local promoters. They in turn seeded accounts with Informix's products.

- *Hardware Partners.* Hewlett-Packard, Sun, IBM, and Digital were the major hardware players of the day. Unfortunately, they were much more interested in working with Oracle and Sybase than with Informix. However, Informix did have reseller relationships with second-tier players such as Sequent, Pyramid, Unisys, Data General, AT&T, NCR, and Bull. Their salespeople were eager to work with us and introduce us into their accounts.

- *UNIX Zealots.* UNIX purists loved Informix. Usually, these people were low-level technical "geeks" within a customer's IT department. Oracle and Sybase would consciously ignore them. Although selling at low levels is risky, surprisingly often these low-level technical people were the ultimate decision makers in many accounts. We befriended them whereas Oracle salespeople ran them over in their haste to get into the CIO's office.

- *The Outcasts and Ignored.* "People don't buy from people they have never met" was an important Informix concept. Therefore, we went out of our way to meet and educate potential customers about UNIX and Informix. Our goal was to be the first database salesperson to start a relationship with a customer.

I'll never forget taking my presales engineer on a sales call to the system manager of a restaurant chain. About ten minutes into our presentation, the customer interrupted with a basic question. Almost everyone in IT should have known the answer: "What's client-server?" After the call, my engineer berated me for taking him on such a worthless call. However, I argued we had found the perfect account because these customers would surely need someone to handhold them through their migration to Open Systems. We sold them $50,000 of software shortly thereafter. In essence, we were the kinder, nicer, and easier-to-deal-with company. This was not because we necessarily wanted to be but because the circumstances of the day dictated it.

## SURVIVING 1991, LOOKING FORWARD TO 1992

Selling Informix was difficult in 1991. We were the underdogs with a subpar product, and the momentum was clearly in favor of our competition. A newsgroup posting accurately reflects the difficulty of the Informix decision: "Buying Informix was a tough decision. There are a number of good databases for the IBM RS 6000 including Oracle, Sybase, Ingres, and Unify. The version purchased was 4.0 and based on that version, it looked like Informix was not as technically current as Ingres and Sybase. I had heard, however, that Informix planned a major new release by the end of the year which would put it on par or perhaps ahead of the competition."[25]

However, this period of hardship was actually a blessing in disguise for the sales organization. It created the culture of partnering and honed our competitive skills. One of the main reasons for our future success was that this core group of battle-hardened salespeople stayed together almost completely intact for the following five years.

At the time, we had no doubt that the Informix sales organization was better than Oracle's or Sybase's, and the financial numbers back up these claims. Even with inferior products, Informix sales rose from $146 million in 1990 to $180 million in 1991. Earnings per share went from a twenty-three-cent loss a year before to a ten-cent gain.[26] The stock surged 448 percent, and Informix was ranked number one by the *San Francisco Chronicle* in total return to investors for the year.[27]

At Informix, we felt a sense of optimism about the future. The market for UNIX was heating up, and we were about to release a new version of our database. Informix finally started to receive some positive press, and the November issue of *Computerworld* magazine made these comments about the next database release: "The Informix 5.0 Engine will, for the first time, support two-phase commit, which enforces proper updates, and stored procedures, which enforce consistent data values. Both features are key because Ingres and Sybase support them now, and Oracle is set to deliver them with version 7.0 in 1992."[28] Above all else, we had faith in the company and its leadership.

## LESSONS LEARNED FROM 1991

For Informix, 1991 had been a tenuous year. Informix had survived a failed merger, competitive disadvantages, and the uphill battle against Oracle and Sybase. It was also a year of transition. Phil White had established himself as a leader who was unafraid to make the tough decisions necessary to get the company back on track. While the future looked promising, no one really knew how bright it would be. Looking back, I see four major business and leadership lessons to be learned from Informix Software and Phil White in 1991.

- People will endure hardships and difficult situations as long as they have faith in the company's leadership and hope for the future. Informix's employees had faith in Phil White.

He commanded their respect not solely by the authority of his title but by the power of his presence.

- There's no such thing as a friendly merger. Informix's merger with Innovative cost the company time and money and wasted energy. More importantly, it defocused the company from its core business. Similarly, Ingres's merger with Ask Computer Systems created doubts about the future of their products. As a result, potential buyers were not interested in evaluating their technology and focused their research on Oracle, Sybase, and Informix.

- Most high-technology customers make up their minds very early in the sales cycle as to which product they will buy. As a result, whether inadvertently or on purpose, customers will always lie to the nonpreferred vendors. A salesperson's job is to find the ultimate truth—"Will I win the deal?"— as soon as possible.

- When understaffed and technically outclassed, you must carefully choose the battles you fight, and it makes no sense to fight them alone. Informix truly believed in partnering because it was the only way to compete with the behemoth Oracle and technically superior Sybase.

*People naturally fear misfortune and long for good fortune; but if the distinction is carefully studied, misfortune often turns to be good fortune and good fortune to be misfortune. The wise man learns to meet the changing circumstances of life with an equitable spirit, neither elated by success nor depressed by failure.*

BUDDHA

# 2

# Phil's War Strategy
## 1992

*Wars may be fought with weapons but they are won by men.*
*It is the spirit of the men who follow and the man who leads*
*that gains victory.*

GENERAL GEORGE S. PATTON

Scientists believe that one of the major differences that separated human beings from the rest of the animal world is the fact that we waged war. War is thought to be a uniquely human trait. War isn't instinctual; it's something people choose to do. War also has a nasty habit of bringing out the worst in those who are involved.

In 1992 there were many wars within the computer industry: Sun's sparring against Next, the ongoing battle between Microsoft Windows and IBM's OS/2, and the price war between Compaq and IBM in the PC market. None of these battles came close in intensity to the one between Oracle and Sybase. Both companies released increasingly confrontational advertisements that stirred up a desire for revenge on both sides. Industry publications continually added fuel to the war fires when they published blow-by-blow exchanges between the companies. The following quotes are from a *UnixWorld* magazine article titled "Who Says the Hostilities Are Over?"

Mark Hoffmann, Sybase Inc.'s President commenting on Larry Ellison, CEO of Oracle, "Larry Ellison? . . . I find nothing attractive about anything I've heard about him. Oracle has a lot of blemishes. It has a whole culture turn around him."

Oracle's vice president of relational database management system marketing instilling fear, uncertainty, and doubt about Sybase, "Sybase is the Wizard of Oz of database companies. I'm hearing some sad stories about Sybase being overextended."

Sybase's director of product management, talking about Oracle's lack of integrity, "We're not the sleazes that Oracle is."

Oracle's senior director of corporate strategy on Sybase's continual attacks on Oracle's professionalism, "Sybase likes to characterize us as the Death Star and Larry Ellison as Darth Vader. Since Sybase's IPO, it's gone from the innocence of childhood to the surly aggressiveness of a 14-year-old boy."

Sybase's vice president of strategic marketing comparing Sybase's reputation against Oracle's, "When we talk about integrity and ethics, we really mean it."[1]

At Informix, we read these exchanges with mixed feelings. On the one hand, we would have liked to have been mentioned in the same breath as Oracle and Sybase. On the other hand, the negativity of the fighting between the companies was mutually destructive. It put off potential customers and made their business partners uncomfortable. This provided an opportunity for Informix to continue to differentiate itself as the friendlier and classier database alternative. Moreover, Sybase and Oracle were too busy attacking each other to bother with Informix. Being left out of the fray actually helped Informix. It provided us with the time to catch up technically and the opportunity to execute Phil's war strategy.

In addition, the database market was quickly consolidating so that potential customers evaluated only the "big three": Oracle,

Sybase, and Informix. Industry trade magazines further accelerated the compression by reporting only on the news of the big three. Ingres, Progress, Empress, Interbase, and Foxpro suddenly found themselves relegated to small niches far from the mainstream of buyer activity and out of the main battle for the database market.

## THE DBMS BATTLEGROUND

The DBMS war was being fought for a huge prize. By the end of the decade, the worldwide DBMS market would be an $8-billion-a-year business.[2] The victor would own the future rights to supply databases for the decade's major IT movements: the downsizing from mainframes, business process engineering, the Internet, and Y2K (the change from the year 1999 to 2000 that was expected to wreak havoc on computer systems).

Most of the world's business information at the time was stored on mainframe computers. The software applications running on these mainframes were developed in the 1960s and 1970s. They were difficult to change and more expensive to maintain than applications for the new, state-of-the-art programming environments available. The cost savings were huge motivators for companies to move legacy applications to UNIX.

As industry momentum continued to build for UNIX, users of proprietary systems increasingly found that software tools and business applications weren't being ported to their minicomputer systems (or the ports weren't available until a year or two later). In addition, the technical talent pool (programmers, operators, and systems personnel) wanted to work on the platforms that were considered "hot." Recruiting quality technical talent to work on non-UNIX platforms became increasingly more difficult.

Another big change to the industry was caused by the rise of the PC. According to the market research firm Dataquest, worldwide sales of PCs reached $47 billion in 1992.[3] Home computer users entered and retrieved information using a mouse and a graphical user interface provided by Microsoft or Apple. Meanwhile, workplace applications were character-based applications on dumb terminals. The user community applied incredible pressure on IT departments to provide a new generation of applications that were not only easier to use but more aesthetic. As a result, client-server computing, the ability for a personal computer to request information from a backend server, took off.

Another extension of client-server computing was the point-and-click analysis of large volumes of data that had been offloaded from a mainframe to a high-performance UNIX machine. Data warehousing and EIS (executive information systems) provided easy-to-use interfaces that executives could use to analyze and drill down on data. Each of these support systems required relational databases.

In April 1992, AMR Research wrote its first report on an obscure German software company called "SAP" (Systems Analysis and Program Development). SAP would offer the first truly client-server Open Systems-based enterprise application. SAP introduced the world to a new generation of enterprise client-server applications. In addition to PeopleSoft and Oracle, these enterprise application vendors would become key enablers of the business process reengineering mania that swept the Fortune 1000 companies starting in 1993. Relational database technology was the foundation of all of these enterprise applications.

Even in 1992, companies were worried about the date change at the end of the millennium and the necessity to modify outdated systems. Y2K became the impetus to migrate many antiquated applications to UNIX and client-server systems. It also served as a prime motivator for businesses to implement state-of-the-art applications from SAP and PeopleSoft.

No one could have correctly predicted the impact of the Internet in 1992. In fact, it would be two years until UNIX pioneer Sun Microsystems launched its external Web site Sun.com. Exceeding everyone's wildest expectations, the Internet would soon hit the world full force. All Web sites would require databases to store content, catalog, and e-commerce information.

UNIX would become the primary platform used for each of these diverse initiatives. Because of its flexibility and adaptability it became the de facto standard. Denis Richie, author of the C programming language and one of the original developers of UNIX, called it "the Swiss army knife of software. UNIX is simple and coherent, but it takes a genius (or at any rate a programmer) to understand and appreciate the simplicity."[4] Just as UNIX had changed the computing landscape, Phil White was making a tumultuous change at Informix.

## A NEW BUSINESS MODEL, MISSION STATEMENT, AND CEO ROLE

Upon joining Informix, Phil had to fight a war on several fronts. There was the pressing war against Oracle and Sybase. Organizationally, there was the fight to right a company that had been taken off course by a bad merger. Because of divisive internal politics, he needed to create a new Informix that was separate from the past. To do so, he would have to make changes to the board of directors, the management team, and even the way the company accounted for revenues.

Adding to the complexity of the situation was that the company's founder continued to wander the Informix hallways. Sippl was known as a genuinely nice guy who was extremely well liked by the employees. In contrast, Phil was a no-nonsense businessman who demanded respect. As long as Sippl was an active part of the day-to-day business, employees would always have a shadow of doubt that Phil's authority was absolute. They would be able to take their complaints and protests about Phil's hardhearted decisions directly to Sippl.

Vast personal differences existed between Phil and Sippl, and the changing role of the CEO reflected this. Phil was the consummate networker. At the end of every quarter, Phil would write almost one thousand handwritten notes, add them to a press release announcing the quarter's results, and send them to industry colleagues. The former high school drama student enjoyed being in the public eye and relished the role of company spokesperson. Just as he had given tours of exotic locations while in college, he now gave verbal tours of Informix's company strategy and product vision to industry analysts and press. Since Phil was a salesman at heart, he enjoyed making sales calls. Helping the sales force was always his top priority.

Phil reinvigorated the executive team with a group of experienced leaders. His first hire was Ira Dorf as vice president of human resources. Phil had been introduced to him in the past and was particularly impressed with his ability to recruit senior executives, a skill he knew he needed. Next, he brought on Howard Graham as CFO. Graham was his trusted advisor and friend from Wyse. He retooled sales management with two seasoned executives, Edwin Winder and Frank Bergandi. As the company grew, he split marketing into corporate and field functions and brought in marketing expert Steve Sommer to complement Bob Macdonald.

He also brought in several senior executives who shared his IBM background. Mike Saranga joined as vice president of research and development. Saranga was widely known in the database industry from his association with IBM's DB2, the most widely used mainframe database in the world. Informix's marketing collateral credited him as the inventor of DB2. Perhaps Phil's most critical hire was to fill one of the most unglamorous positions. To fix the technical support quagmire, he brought in Jim Hendrickson as vice president of customer services, who turned around the support operations.

While Phil's background was sales and marketing, he acted more like a bean counter who was fixated on expense control. "Controlling expenses is a crucial factor in running a successful company," he said in a *San Jose Mercury News* article.[5] Expense control was a constant subject on Phil's frugal mind. "Phil White knows how to run a software firm like a business," a Dataquest analyst said later in the same article. Along the walls of the Informix hallways, charts were continually posted showing the latest financial figures and revenue and spending trends. The most important of these charts recorded revenue per employee, calculated by dividing total revenues by the number of employees. Human capital is the most expensive part of any software company, and Phil used this metric to keep the headcount as low as possible. He wanted Informix staffing to be intentionally lean when it came to nondevelopment and non-revenue-generating positions.

The new Informix financial model Phil put in place was intentionally simple. The goal of the company was to clear a 20 percent pretax quarterly profit. This goal drove the company's business plans and actions. Phil commented, "The beauty about having a simple business model is that everyone understands it and knows how to be measured and potentially get paid. For every dollar of revenue, we are going to spend 50 percent of it on worldwide sales and marketing, 10 percent on cost of goods, 10 percent on R&D and 10 percent on overhead. That leaves 20 percent pretax."[6] He frequently repeated this business mantra to employees, customers, partners, and the press.

Accompanying the new business model was a new attitude. The "new" Informix persona reflected Phil's low-key demeanor. "When I took over as CEO I knew Informix was going through some serious problems, but I was calm," he would later say about the critical time of Informix.[7] Informix would not practice high-pressure sales or overhype its products, as was common within the software industry. We were going to take the moral high ground in the database market. Being low-key didn't mean the company wasn't tenacious or aggressive; it meant that we wouldn't broadcast our punches before we threw them. Informix would be the confident, calm company.

The culture within Informix would be casual. The tone was set by the way everyone in the company called Phil by his first name. He in turn called everyone by his or her last name, reflecting his desire to treat everyone the same. Regardless of whether you were a salesperson or a vice president, he would say, "Hey, Martin!" or "What's new, Bergandi?"

Perhaps Phil's most pressing problem was the composition of the board of directors. Two of the directors were the result of the Innovative merger. In order to fix the company, he centralized important operations in Menlo Park. He pronounced it the worldwide headquarters and relegated Lenexa to support and manufacturing functions. Within a year and a half, the Innovative board members left on their own and he was able to bring in his own people. He had eased out the Innovative members over time instead of forcing them out through confrontation.

Phil considered keeping the board members happy and keeping them informed as two of his primary duties. Although the board members received a domestic update at every board meeting in Menlo Park, Phil wanted them to understand the worldwide nature of Informix's business. Every year, he took the board members and their wives on an all-expenses-paid trip to a five-star international resort. They traveled to Tokyo, London, Munich, Mexico City, Singapore, and Mexico. While their wives shopped and pampered themselves, the board members listened to presentations from the local management, held press conferences, and met with dignitaries. Far more important than these official duties were the personal friendships that formed on these junkets. The board liked and trusted Phil.

In addition to keeping the board happy, Phil worked hard to make sure our partners were happy too. Getting our partners to like us not only was common sense, but it was a survival strategy. The old saying "There's safety in numbers" was definitely true for Informix. Informix surrounded itself with business partners that had a stake in Informix's success. When Informix won business, our partners won financially by selling their products and services or reselling ours. Partners were a fundamental ingredient in our strategy to defeat Oracle and Sybase.

The company adopted a new mission statement with partnerships as the central theme. While other members of the senior staff had wanted the mission statement to focus mainly on technology, Phil dictated that the phrase "through partnerships worldwide" be included in the mission statement: "The mission of Informix is to provide, through partnerships worldwide, the best technology and services for developing enterprise-wide data management applications."[8]

Just as Intel had launched its "Intel inside" campaign, Phil announced the "Built with Informix" campaign. The goal was for Informix to become ubiquitous, everywhere all at once. The only way to accomplish this goal was to offer partners and customers a product line that they could use selectively or all together, in small increments or across the board.

## A LINE OF PRODUCTS VERSUS A PRODUCT LINE

Many technology companies sell a line of products, but very few sell a product line. While both can be targeted at a certain market or a set of particular users within an IT organization, a product line is different in that it fits together and encourages the use of other products in the line. The only way to compete against Oracle and Sybase was by offering not just superior technology but an entire product line that fit our partners' business models. More importantly, a product line lets the user start small, validate that the technology and the company support work as advertised, and then increase the scope and magnitude of usage over time.

The Informix product line was synchronized to the UNIX marketplace. One of Informix's first products was C-ISAM, nonrelational indexed sequential file system. This was the first ISAM file product available for UNIX. Consequently, it was used almost everywhere and embedded in software, operating systems, and hardware devices. Even

Oracle used it at one time. The nice part about C-ISAM was that users could install the Informix Standard Engine relational database on top of C-ISAM and instantly add relational capabilities to their C-ISAM-based applications. Standard Engine was an easy-to-use, low-maintenance, SQL (structured query language) compliant database that required minimal administration.

The UNIX marketplace is based upon the C programming language, which was originally developed to write and implement the UNIX operating system. ESQL-C (embedded SQL for C) was Informix's product that enabled SQL statements to be embedded within C programs. However, C is arduous to write and difficult to learn. Informix offered 4GL software that enabled tenfold productivity over C. It was an English-like procedural language that generated C code. Because of this, even hard-core UNIX programmers liked it. Sybase didn't offer a programming environment anything like 4GL.

Informix OnLine was our flagship database and what people thought of first when asked if they were using Informix. OnLine was a high-performance, mission-critical database used for deploying large online transaction-processing applications and as the repository for huge amounts of data. We also referred to OnLine as our "database engine." Technically, the portion of the database that is truly the engine is the part that performs data insertion and deletion operations on database tables. However, over time the term "engine" became synonymous and completely interchangeable with the word "database."

You could administer both Standard Engine and Informix OnLine through the same interface using I-SQL (Informix SQL). Also, ESQL-C and Informix 4GL programs would run against either database interchangeably. Therefore, once a user had installed Standard Engine, the upsell to OnLine was easy since the benefits were immediate.

The product line was a key differentiator against Oracle and Sybase. Informix offered a low-end, small-footprint database to start on. Value-added resellers (VARs) loved it because it was inexpensive and easy to administer. Customers liked it because as their processing requirements grew they could seamlessly migrate applications to its big-brother database, mission-critical OnLine. Since both databases were administered via the same interface, customers could deploy them in a mix-and-match methodology. For example, a nationwide retailer might put Standard Engine at the retail stores and OnLine at the corporate offices to process the stores' data.

Most importantly to the Informix sales organization, customers would usually buy the entire suite of products together. Even though customers would initially be looking only for a database, they almost always bought all of the other products since they were so complementary. This made not only the deal bigger but Informix's role in the IT organization more significant. Application developers in addition to database administrators would be introduced to our products. It was a self-perpetuating cycle. As the developers built more applications they would buy more databases.

This cycle gave Informix the ability to lock Oracle and Sybase out of an account while maximizing revenues. During this time frame, growing revenues were crucial because customers would evaluate only the largest vendors. However, what constituted legitimate software license revenues was still under debate.

## INFORMIX'S FIRST REVENUE RESTATEMENT

Oracle's near bankruptcy in 1990 frightened the entire software industry. It made customers nervous and software companies apprehensive. The rationale was, if Oracle could go out of business, it could happen to anyone. The crisis came about because of the tactics used by Oracle's sales force, which were (and remain today) commonplace in the industry. The salespeople subscribed to an "up-front" sales strategy, in which they tried to incent customers to buy the biggest amounts of software all at once.

What makes this strategy dangerous is how the payments for the software are made. When a payment is made up-front, the cash coming in from the sale matches the company's stated revenue. However, Oracle used extended multiyear payment terms and huge volume purchase discounts to motivate customers to make the biggest possible purchases. Unfortunately, the software business is a risky one to be in because software doesn't always work. Oracle's software was no exception to this rule. Also, the software promised to customers in many cases was actually "vaporware"—it didn't exist. Unhappy customers will use whatever means possible to express their frustration, and the most effective is to stop making payments. Ultimately, most of these debts go uncollected and accounting receivables balloon.

In 1990, Oracle took a $12.4 million loss and laid off 10 percent of the work force because of the mismatch between cash and revenues. Oracle also had to restate earnings twice. The company would later pay $24 million to settle class-action lawsuits that had been filed because of its flawed financial statements.[9] Larry Ellison would later say his company made "an incredible business mistake."[10] The company instituted new revenue recognition policies and reined in its renegade sales force.

When the American Institute of Certified Public Accountants issued a more conservative statement on software revenue recognition in 1991, Phil voluntarily put the more stringent recommendations in practice. "Everybody's going to have to get more conservative," he said in an *Information Week* article.[11] An IT executive at one of Informix's key installations, Citicorp in New York, was quoted as saying at the time, "We met them and reviewed all the issues. It was prudent that Informix was a leader in revamping its financial practices."[12]

Before the change of policy, Informix would recognize revenue on contracts with terms up to twenty-four months. For example, if a creditworthy customer signed a nonrefundable contract to purchase $400,000 of software and agreed to make eight quarterly payments of $50,000, the entire $400,000 would be recognized as a sale at the time the contract was signed. The more conservative policy would recognize only revenue for the first twelve months.

Making this revenue accounting change would force Informix to restate its 1990 earnings and increase the annual loss to $42 million. However, the $42 million did not really disappear. It would be recognized as revenue as it accrued later. Phil commented about the loss to *Upside Magazine:* "It was a $40 million loss for a company that was doing $150 million in revenue. It was a paper loss—we literally were debooking the revenue and moving it out into the future."[13] Phil had made a conscious decision to make the 1990 loss as big as possible in order to improve the odds for long-term success. Six years later, history would repeat itself when the new president of Informix made revenue recognition even more conservative. Symbolically, the 1997 restatement also marked the end of Informix's war against Oracle.

## VERSION WAR

The ammunition each database vendor used to fight the database war was the latest version of its database. As a new release nears completion, it is called an "alpha" version. Since it has limited functionality and crashes often, the first working release is used internally to test the product. The software moves into a "beta" version as the product matures and bugs are worked out. While this version still contains defects and some features aren't fully implemented, it is released to selected customers who volunteer to serve as "guinea pigs." After a successful beta test is performed, the product then becomes available to the general public.

The numbering scheme used by most software companies is to place the number of the major version followed by a decimal point and the number of the minor version (5.1, 6.2, 7.3, and so on). The first number represents major changes and improvements. This typically indicates a completely new architecture or many enhanced features. Minor versions are bug fixes or minor enhancements to the major version. For example, 4.9 means "major version 4, minor version 9." In addition, every time the source code is modified, it is numbered to reflect the revision. The complete version number of a product is expressed as major.minor.revision (e.g., 4.9.5 or 7.2.02).

In 1992, Informix unveiled the latest release of its database, Informix OnLine 5.0. (Prior to Phil's joining Informix the database had been called "Turbo." He renamed the product "OnLine.") OnLine version 5.0 was a godsend to the sales force. It included features such as triggers and stored procedures. Now we could finally go toe-to-toe technically against Oracle and Sybase in the large accounts.

Buying a database was hard work for customers. Customers would research each of the products in industry magazines and newsgroups and use these sources to create a checklist of features. In 1992, the available releases for the "big three" database vendors were Oracle7 (version 7.0), Sybase version 4.9, and Informix OnLine 5.0. Table 3 is a small sample of a matrix to provide some idea of the depth of technical discussions that were made on sales calls. The first column describes a particular database feature or function. The columns under each vendor reflect whether the feature or function is contained within the specific release.

These are just a few of the hundreds of topics customers may have asked about. Also, make a special note of the first feature listed. We didn't know it at the time, but Sybase's lack of support for row-level locking would come back to haunt the company and nearly destroy it.

The last feature was also very important. In 1989, the American National Standards Institute (ANSI) published an SQL specification for accessing and manipulating databases that was independent of any specific DBMS implementation. Adhering to ANSI SQL ensured customers that any application could be migrated from Oracle to Informix, Sybase to Oracle, or vice versa without reengineering. Since

**Table 3.** Vendor Database Feature and Function Checklist

|                                      | *Oracle* | *Sybase* | *Informix* |
|--------------------------------------|----------|----------|------------|
| *Feature or function*                | *7.0*    | *4.9*    | *5.0*      |
| Row-level locking                    | Y        | N        | Y          |
| Page-level locking                   | N        | Y        | Y          |
| Table-level locking                  | Y        | Y        | Y          |
| Database-level locking               | Y        | Y        | Y          |
| Programmable read isolation levels   | N        | N        | Y          |
| Lock escalation                      | Y        | Y        | Y          |
| Dirty read mode                      | N        | N        | Y          |
| Multiserver architecture             | Y        | Y        | N          |
| Symmetric multiprocessor support     | Y        | Y        | Y          |
| Shared commits                       | Y        | Y        | Y          |
| Asynchronous I/O                     | Y        | Y        | Y          |
| Raw I/O                              | Y        | Y        | Y          |
| Shared log files                     | Y        | Y        | Y          |
| Clustered indexes                    | Y        | Y        | Y          |
| Backward-scrolling cursors           | N        | N        | N          |
| Nonblocking sequence generator       | Y        | N        | Y          |
| Unique-key generator                 | Y        | N        | Y          |
| Cost-based optimizer                 | Y        | Y        | Y          |
| Optimizer moves join location        | Y        | N        | Y          |
| Stored procedures in database        | Y        | Y        | Y          |
| Shared cached procedures             | Y        | Y        | N          |
| Stored functions in database         | Y        | N        | Y          |
| Programmer-defined data types        | N        | Y        | N          |
| Supports ANSI SQL                    | Y        | Y        | Y          |

UNIX customers liked the vendor independence SQL offered, they were hesitant to adopt any one vendor's proprietary access methodology. We would find this out at Informix a couple of years later when we acquired Illustra.

We learned another fundamental lesson about customers from these checklist evaluations: 80 percent of all customers would end up using only 20 percent of the product's functionality. Customers would ask questions about features they didn't understand. Sometimes they would say a certain feature was absolutely mandatory when they didn't even know how to use it. Most often, this type of feature discussion was just a red herring to hide the fact that they had already made up their minds in favor of another vendor. Therefore, it was critical not just to answer their questions but more importantly to ask questions about what they thought the feature did, why it was important to them, and how they planned to use it.

Ultimately, customers would learn from their paper evaluations that all three products were very similar in functionality. Each had its own pluses and minuses. Since there wasn't a clear technical leader, how would customers decide which product to buy?

## WHERE WE LOST AND WHERE WE WON

After completing many of these customer checklist evaluations, we noticed a pattern that was analogous to the way people buy cars. All cars perform the same task: they take you from one place to another. However, some people buy practical Chevys, others like the prestige of a Mercedes, and some prefer sporty Porsches. Some loyal Chevy owners buy only American cars, and some Mercedes and Porsche owners never drive anything else. Also, plenty of people would love to drive a Mercedes or a Porsche but simply can't afford one.

In the world of databases, Informix was the Chevy, Oracle the Mercedes, and Sybase the Porsche. Determining whether a decision maker was more likely to be a Mercedes, Porsche, or Chevy buyer greatly cut down on the time wasted trying to sell Informix to companies that would never buy.

It was fairly easy to spot the accounts where Oracle had the advantage and was destined to win. These businesses were looking to standardize on one database for every computer platform they owned or needed extensive mainframe connectivity. Usually, they were already using Oracle at another location or division in the company. Finally, they were the big, worldwide Fortune 1000 companies that were used to dealing with major technology vendors and consulting firms.

Hard-core Windows development shops usually chose Sybase. From our standpoint, it seemed that Microsoft and Sybase had some kind of special relationship. This was in part because Microsoft's SQL Server database was built with Sybase's source code. In 1992, Windows developers were enamored with Microsoft's Visual Basic or Powersoft's graphical application tool, PowerBuilder. These tools supported the native Windows environment and worked best with Sybase. At the time, many people within the industry thought Microsoft would acquire Sybase. However, Sybase would later go on to acquire Powersoft in 1995.

Informix appealed to more frugal companies that ran leaner IT operations. When measured as a percentage of company revenues, these companies' IT budgets were 30 to 50 percent under industry averages. As a result, their IT departments were typically understaffed and underfunded in comparison to the projects they had to accomplish. They needed inexpensive, easy-to-use products that fit within their budget and staffing constraints.

Since the technical functionality among products was now equivalent, the salespeople played a more important role in winning new customers. In fact, the salesperson became the key differentiator because customers would adhere to "The better person syndrome." According to this theory of mine, when customers are choosing between two similar products, they will not always buy the best product. Rather, they will buy from the salesperson who they believe is the better person. So while one salesperson may have a slightly better product and be more proficient in explaining its features and functionality, in the end the customer will buy from the person who better matches the personal attributes that the customer admires and feels comfortable with.

Some evaluators gravitated to the friendly and responsive Informix salesperson, while others gravitated to the aristocratic (from our standpoint) Sybase salesperson. Others seemed to enjoy being around the "slick" salesperson in the cufflinks and monogrammed dress shirt from Oracle. Perhaps these technical decision makers had some deep-seated desire to be like them.

The ultimate factor determining whether Informix won or lost a deal was this: was the salesperson able to build a personal friendship with the customer? For many years, the term "coach" has been used by all types of salespeople, selling every conceivable product, to define the person within the customer's company who is on the salesperson's side and helps him or her win the deal. Where we had a coach, we almost always won. The incredible growth of Informix was due to our ability to build personal relationships with customers and partners. This sales culture was a fundamental part of Phil's strategy. However, these relationships would be tested over the years when our software products didn't work as promised.

## 911 FOR ONLINE 5.0!

The new Informix OnLine version 5.0 had only one problem: it didn't always work. The initial customer installations were problematic. The product frequently crashed and the new features didn't function as expected. To compound the problem, the Informix support center in Lenexa wasn't prepared to handle the issues. It was a volatile situation. We finally had a product that enabled us to win accounts in direct competition with Oracle and Sybase. If these newly won accounts stopped our implementation and switched products, it would be a disaster. The competition would be quick to highlight our failures. If the industry press heard about the product problems, the entire company would be crippled.

The unheralded heroes during the crisis were our presales system engineers. The presales engineers worked hand in hand with the field salespeople in the local sales offices. While they were responsible for presenting Informix's technology and demonstrating software to prospective customers, the presales engineers also took on the burden of handling customers' escalating needs for support since Informix's support center was woefully ineffective.

The engineers would spend hours and sometimes days on-site with customers, debugging software and installing patches. Their presence provided a sense of comfort to the nervous decision makers who had just put their careers on the line by recommending Informix. During these crisis periods, they soothed frayed nerves and built lasting personal relationships. The quality of the technical people in the field was one of the key differentiators between Informix and Oracle and Sybase both before and after a sale.

Surviving the OnLine 5.0 technical fiasco was a significant moment in the company's history, but it was nowhere near as important as what would happen at the end of 1992.

## RCAS: THE INFORMIX TIPPING POINT

In Malcom Gladwell's book *The Tipping Point,* the author explains that major changes in our society happen suddenly and unexpectedly. "Ideas, behavior, messages, and products often spread like an infectious disease. Just as a single person can start the epidemic of the flu, so too can fare-beaters and graffiti artists start a crime wave, or a satisfied customer fill the tables of a new restaurant. These are social epidemics and the moment they take off, when they reach their critical mass, is the Tipping Point."[14] Informix's tipping point occurred in November 1992.

RCAS, or Reserve Component Automation System, was to be the largest automated data processing system ever built. A project for the U.S. Army Reserve Forces and the Army National Guard, it involved 9,800 sites and 60,000 users and would track 500,000 people and billions of dollars of equipment. Boeing was awarded a $1.6 billion bid to be the project's prime contractor.[15]

Obviously, a project of this magnitude would require lots of large databases. In a football-field-sized computer laboratory, each of the major databases was tested and benchmarked in excruciating detail. Many expressed initial disbelief when the U.S. Army Information Systems Selection and Acquisition Agency announced Informix as the winner. Oracle executives were furious and protested the results, but they weren't able to overturn the decision.

In November, Informix received a $21.8 million payment for the federal software contract. That's when Phil made the extraordinary decision that became Informix's tipping point. He gave every employee, more than 1,300 at the time, from receptionist to vice president, a check for $1,000. What made the bonus even more dramatic was that no grandstanding or gloating announcement came with it. Enclosed within your regular paycheck envelope was a note from Phil about RCAS and a separate check for $1,000. It was a complete surprise.

Almost every member of the executive staff had been dead set against his idea. The opponents argued that it would not result in any significant improvement in employee morale or loyalty. Meanwhile, the board wanted the money taken directly to the bottom line. But Phil would not relent. He knew the impact this decision would have on the company. The president knew his employees, and the boy from Pana certainly knew the value of $1,000.

While the money was obviously important, the gesture itself electrified the entire company. We could not believe our good fortune to work for such an employee-oriented company. Any other software company would have taken the $1.3 million spent on the bonuses to the bottom line so that the quarterly earnings per share could be increased by four or five cents. In reality, the dividends were returned a hundredfold in terms of employee loyalty and morale.

The employees weren't the only ones who were excited; their spouses were equally enthused. This had been one of Phil's motivations in the first place. Working for Informix was hard. We had to put in long hours, and we were the industry underdogs who always had to do more with less. The bonus was another way to ensure that the spouses were pro-Informix and a source of encouragement. An Informix vice president said at the time, "It is a statement of Phil White. He really appreciates the people."[16]

The RCAS sales rep instantly achieved godlike status and Informix immortality. While most of the world thinks salespeople are motivated only by money, great salespeople are equally preoccupied with leaving a legacy that will be remembered within a company. While success is a fleeting, quarter-by-quarter, year-by-year proposition, a legacy can never be taken away. Overnight, the bar had been raised and every salesperson wanted to close the next RCAS-type deal.

The RCAS deal changed the way sales management thought of deals. The RCAS sales rep told me later that he thought he was just a few weeks from being fired before the deal closed. This was because the sales organization model required almost all salespeople to make their quotas in order for the company to make its number. Therefore, the prevailing attitude of sales management was that salespeople who didn't make their quarterly quotas were a liability. In reality, big deals don't happen in a single quarter. The Informix sales force needed to be bigger and the quota divided among different types of salespeople, some covering geographic territories and others focused long-term on large accounts.

The RCAS deal also changed the way members of the sales force thought of themselves. For the first time, Informix had beaten Oracle and Sybase in a major deal. Unfortunately, the deal had one negative by-product for salespeople: a change in the sales commission program.

At the beginning of every year, each salesperson was presented a compensation plan ("comp plan") that outlined his or her territory as well as quota and the commission and bonus structure. The comp plan was very generous once salespeople attained their annual quotas. The commission rates increased exponentially, and bonuses were awarded at milestones. For example, for salespeople who made their quotas (typically around $1.8 million in sales), the average on-target earnings (salary plus commissions and bonuses) were around $180,000. However, if they were able to sell twice their quotas, they would make around $400,000.

Given the comp plan's formulas, the RCAS sales rep would have made millions of dollars on the deal. However, Informix reserved the right to change the comp plan at any time. Sales operations added what the sales reps called the "RCAS clause." The company had the prerogative to review large-revenue transactions and increase the quota, change the commission rate, or make other adjustments it considered to be fair and reasonable. Informix now could pay commissions on very large deals at the discretion of the regional vice president of sales.

## ALL THE TITLES

Phil got an early Christmas gift at the end of 1992 when Roger Sippl decided to resign his position as chairman of the board and pass it on to Phil. Sippl's decision to leave was not an easy one. He elaborated upon his resignation: "I suspect it's always difficult for a founder to leave, and it is certainly true in my case. However, since the company has enjoyed record-breaking revenues and profits, and has the best balance sheet in its history, I have no problem leaving the company. I give credit to Phil White and to the officers and employees of Informix for an outstanding financial turnaround."[17]

Now everything was in place: Phil had all the titles (president, CEO, and chairman), held all the power, and had a board of directors that was to his liking. The company was gathering momentum. At the end of 1992, Forrester Research projected that within two years 68 percent of the Fortune 1000 would run key database applications on relational database software on smaller UNIX systems.[18] The future looked very bright.

While all the database companies would enjoy the benefits of this mass migration, none was better positioned for success than Informix. A software analyst for Soundview Financial summed it up best when he said, "Informix is at the right place at the right time. The heyday of UNIX is approaching, and Informix is superbly positioned for that."[19]

## LESSONS LEARNED FROM 1992

The turning point for Informix occurred in 1992. The company was gaining momentum and was recognized as the number three provider of database technology behind Oracle and Sybase. While the company was sure to benefit from the growth of UNIX, four important business and leadership lessons can be learned from Informix Software and Phil White in 1992.

- Pick on someone your own size. It would have been senseless for Informix to pick a war with Oracle, a gorilla four times its size. Instead, the company set its sights on Sybase, a competitor that was roughly the same size. In order to gain superiority of numbers, Phil established the partnering as the core philosophy of Informix.

- Know your strengths. From a technical perspective, Informix offered a more complete product line than Sybase. From a personal perspective, customers liked us better. We used these two advantages to differentiate ourselves from our competitors and win over new customers and partners.

- Before you start to fight any war, you need to make sure you are internally prepared to win. Phil retooled the management, the board, and the internal operations within sales, support, and research and development prior to launching the Sybase attack. Equally important, the salespeople (warriors in the field) were given financial incentives to form alliances with partners and work together in order to defeat Sybase.

- Companies can create their own tipping points that will greatly influence their success or failure. The RCAS deal and Phil's decision to give a bonus to every employee unified the company, created an esprit de corps, and fostered a new "anything is possible" culture within Informix.

*Luck or tragedy, some people get runs. Then of course there are those who divide it even, good and bad, but we never hear of them. Such a life doesn't demand attention. Only the people who get the good or bad runs.*

JOHN STEINBECK

# 3

# Reaching the Summit
## 1993–1994

*There are only two ways to live your life. One is as though nothing is a miracle; the other is as though everything is a miracle.*

ALBERT EINSTEIN

Nearly every religion includes the story of a courageous figure climbing a mountaintop to receive wisdom and enlightenment. Throughout history, mountain climbing has become a symbol of achievement, spiritual reward, and physical accomplishment. The eternalness of mountains also reminds us of the fleeting nature of our existence. Their grandeur provides affirmation of our role in the world's grand scheme.

Informix had its own version of the mountaintop experience called "Summit Club." Only the top sales performers from around the world earned a spot for themselves and a guest at Summit Club, this ultraexclusive celebration. The annual event was held at a first-class resort in a different exotic location each year shortly after the sales kickoff. Attendees were given lavish gifts, spending money, and free rein to pamper themselves with massages and facials or enjoy activities such as golf, scuba diving, and helicopter rides.

Summit Club was Phil's personal party. He was intimately involved in the planning, from the decision on where it was held to the gifts each person received nightly. A consummate host, he personally approved the list of attendees. He wanted every detail to be perfect and the experience to be long remembered. He knew the opulence of the Summit Club event would be the topic of company conversations for months. He was also aware that one of the most frequent questions salespeople would ask of each other throughout the year was, "Do you think you will make Summit Club?"

To become a leader within Informix you had to attain Summit Club. Summit Club established the sales organization's pecking order. Regardless of how many times you had attended in the past, you weren't considered a player unless you attended the most recent one. Therefore, Summit Club motivated the sales force just as much as the comp plan. Aside from the recognition, it was the only time you could socialize with Phil and fraternize with the company's executive staff in a nonwork setting.

The final night of the three-day event was always very special. In 1993, the event was held in Puerto Rico. On a tropical beach attendees dined on steak and lobster and drank the best wines. Against a throbbing backdrop of Jamaican music, mingling with the audience were live entertainers: limbo artists, snake charmers, and tarot readers. Then Phil announced he had one more surprise and asked everyone to follow him on a walk down the beach. On his command, the sky lit up with explosions and the most spectacular fireworks show followed. The climax was "INFORMIX" spelled out in blazing twenty-foot-high letters.

## PHIL WHITE'S FIREWORKS

However, the real fireworks were just starting for Informix. If you had bought $32,000 worth of Informix stock at its low in 1991, it would have been worth a million dollars at its 1993 high.[1] Informix was ranked as the number one company for return on equity by the *San Jose Mercury News* in its annual Silicon Valley 150.[2] With profits up 349 percent, Informix was ranked number three in the *Los Angeles Times* top 100 California companies.[3] One of Phil's favorite financial measuring sticks, revenue per employee, was up 70 percent from 1990—to $185,000 per employee.[4]

Phil was proclaimed a Silicon Valley hero. The press printed articles about Informix with titles and subtitles that included "Analysts Credit Informix CEO with Silicon Valley Success Story"[5] and "Informix's Phillip White: Converting Personal Ambition into Companywide Success."[6] In March, Phil was named CEO of the year by *Financial World* magazine.[7]

Phil White also joined the very elite club of highly paid Silicon Valley executives. In 1993, he exercised $3,653,750 of his stock options on top of his $812,212 in salary to become one of the highest-paid executives in the Valley. Newspapers reported the value of his future options at over $17 million.[8] He had risen from relative obscurity to become one of the most recognized businesspeople in Silicon Valley in just four short years.

## SPEED RULES

In 1993, UNIX emerged to become the preferred platform for mission-critical applications that ran day-to-day business operations. Businesses deployed UNIX in seven-by-twenty-four environments, including order-entry systems, inventory management, banking transactions, and telecommunications networks. The failure of any of these systems would have catastrophic results—the inability to conduct business, operational chaos, and the loss of money. UNIX was now considered a mainstream technology.

Now that the feature sets of the Oracle, Informix, and Sybase databases were basically equal, how would customers make their UNIX database selection? In many large accounts the decision was purely political, and IT managers would simply dictate that they were to use Oracle. Outside of these accounts, however, the market displayed a genuine sense of confusion as customers sought to determine which product was truly best.

When Phil was asked how his database stacked up against the competition, his response was, "Our high-end engine is as good as any other. I don't see any difference in our engines. If you take a feature like triggers, stored procedures, or two-phase commit—we all have them."[9] However, the one place where Informix OnLine stood out from the competition was performance, and "performance" would become the new Informix mantra.

From a sales strategy standpoint, Informix shifted the deciding argument from database functionality to speed and ease of use. We encouraged customers to install an evaluation copy of our product, knowing full well that Oracle and Sybase would prefer a paper study versus a product test-drive. We knew our product was easier to install than Sybase's and that it was difficult to get evaluation copies from Oracle. When our competitors didn't readily provide evaluation software to customers, it gave the customers the impression that the companies had something to hide.

From our perspective, it also seemed that both competitors' support desks were understaffed. They obviously didn't want potential customers to find this out before the sale. Conversely, Informix had gone to considerable lengths to improve customer support. New management had been hired, and some of the company's most talented engineers were brought in for tours of duty in technical support.

This sales strategy put both competitors in a bind and helped us gain a position of strength. It was a simple strategy: volunteer evaluation copies early and often in the sales cycle to put competitors on the defensive. The message this sent to customers was that we had total confidence in our product and company. However, we knew we couldn't drop off a copy of our software on the customer's doorstep and expect everything would work out fine. The local sales team had to provide extensive hands-on help and manage the process.

When a customer took us up on our offer, we also benefited because our system engineers would become our on-site eyes and ears within the account. Every salesperson had his or her own system engineer to smother the customer with tender loving care. Since Oracle and Sybase mainly used pools of engineers that their salespeople would draw from, they couldn't provide the same level of personal attention. Meanwhile, we were able to build the deep technical relationships that truly influenced a deal's outcome.

Some customers wanted to benchmark how fast the databases could crunch information. However, it was a fairly laborious project to bring in Oracle, Sybase, and Informix and install and configure each database, import the test data, and tune each database. In addition, most companies didn't have the extra hardware, staff, or network bandwidth to spare. Therefore, real benchmarking occurred infrequently. More often than not, customers would install the software and do some light testing.

In reality, we didn't want to install our products any more than Oracle and Sybase did. Managing evaluations was a time-consuming constraint on the account team's productivity. Therefore, wherever we could, we presented benchmark information to validate our performance claims in an attempt to avoid an evaluation and still claim the performance advantage.

Database software really can't be demonstrated because there really isn't anything to see. It's like shopping for a car. You can open the hood and look at the engine, but you can't see what's happening inside. However, you can compare measurements of car speeds (zero to sixty in sixty seconds, for example) to determine an engine's performance. In the database world, the standardized benchmarks were based upon the Transaction Processing Performance Council's (TPC) guidelines.

Historically, the competition to offer the fastest database as evidenced by the best benchmarks had been intense. The competition began in the early 1980s when manufacturers began to make claims regarding their computer systems' performance. These statements had little credibility in the press and with customers because they were based solely on the vendors' marketing claims. This exaggerated "benchmarketing" also frustrated other vendors when one claimed superior performance based upon questionable tactics.

As a result, eight vendors got together to bring a semblance of law and order to benchmarking. In 1988, they established the Transaction Processing Performance Council, a nonprofit corporation founded to define transaction processing benchmarks and to disseminate objective, verifiable performance data to the industry. The TPC created fair-use policies for its benchmarks. It dictated that when TPC results are used in publicity, the use is "Expected to adhere to basic standards of fidelity, candor, and due diligence."[10]

Completing TPC benchmarks required the cooperation of both a computer hardware vendor and a database company. The companies would spend hundreds of thousands of dollars to create an objective benchmark that would be approved by the council. The results would be measured as the total costs of the hardware and database divided by the number of transactions processed per minute. Hardware vendors wanted to use the fastest and least expensive database. As a result, Informix was the natural choice and was used almost exclusively by all of the hardware vendors.

Informix benefited immensely from the TPC benchmarks since they were aggressively promoted by hardware vendors when they marketed their computers. Of all the various types of benchmarks, the TPC-C (complex online) benchmark was the most coveted. "In the TPC-C benchmarks we won awards with IBM and HP for the largest transactions at the lowest costs," Phil bragged to the media.[11] These benchmarks gave potential customers the impression that IBM, HP, and Sun preferred Informix. In reality, this wasn't always the case in the field.

Since we didn't offer any products for mainframes, most large IT shops didn't know who Informix was. They were familiar only with

Oracle. Having the hardware vendors promote Informix was crucial to increasing our name recognition. When IBM, DEC, HP, and Sun promoted their benchmarks, they introduced us to an entirely new class of customers who would soon be implementing UNIX. The benchmark results were also circulated among technical evaluators through newsgroups and database forums. Here's a typical benchmark press release of the time, issued by Sun Microsystems.[12]

### SPARCSERVER 1000 RUNNING INFORMIX DELIVERS INDUSTRY'S BEST DATABASE PRICE/PERFORMANCE

MOUNTAIN VIEW, Calif.—A Sun® SPARCserver™ 1000 system running the Informix OnLine 5.01 RDBMS offers the best price/performance among all database servers in the industry, based on the Transaction Processing Performance Council benchmark, TPC-C. Among database servers, the SPARCserver 1000 is the fastest available today. The system achieved 1079.43 transactions per minute (tpm) and $1,038 per tpmC, beating all other servers' published results.

Informix was recognized as the fastest database, and this clearly bothered Oracle. Oracle was determined to regain its performance leadership and mysteriously posted some incredible benchmark numbers. However, in April 1993, the Standish Group, a consulting firm that focuses on IT technology investments, charged that Oracle had added a special enhancement called "discrete transaction" to the database solely for benchmarking purposes. Standish argued that this feature "Violated the spirit of the TPC."[13]

The press seized the opportunity to vilify Oracle. *Network World* magazine reported, "Report Finds Oracle TPC Results to be Misleading."[14] Oracle's credibility was damaged and its benchmarks were viewed with suspicion from that point on. Meanwhile, Informix was perceived as the honest company with the fastest database.

Better benchmarks didn't mean we would win every deal, but it certainly helped our visibility. But the biggest surprise was Sybase and that their database was absent from the TPC's benchmark reports. One might assume its product didn't scale well. It was only a matter of time before this deficiency would become public and haunt the company.

## SYBASE'S FIRST MISSTEP

Sybase had adopted an aggressive acquisition strategy, and the effects of its acquisition of Gain Software in late 1992 sapped the company's focus. Gain was a developer of multimedia application development tools, and the merger's goal was to be able to offer application development tools that were commensurate to those offered by Informix and Oracle.

When Phil was asked if he would have bought Gain, he said, "No. The tool is not well integrated. If you wrote stuff with Sybase's old tools and switched to Gain, you would have to rewrite all that stuff."[15] The merger was ultimately a bust, and *DBMS Magazine* later wrote, "Sybase essentially dumped its own application development tool strategy, which was based around the Gain tools."[16] At Informix, we started to think that perhaps Sybase wasn't as invincible as it had once seemed.

Customers typically experience a long lag time between selecting a database and actually deploying it. It's not uncommon for a company to take up to a year to build the application, install the computers and networking equipment, and then roll out the application to the end users. As a result, the customer doesn't truly know if the database software works until long after it is purchased.

In mid-1993, we started to hear rumblings from disgruntled Sybase customers who had previously evaluated Informix. They were unhappy with the performance of Sybase's database and frustrated with its support organization. Customers who had paid hundreds of thousands of dollars to Sybase were now second-guessing their decision.

Sybase had released a new version of its flagship database. The company had rearchitected the software and released it as Sybase System 10. Unlike Informix and Oracle, which numbered releases sequentially, Sybase felt its next-generation database deserved special merit, so the number jumped from version four to ten. The first users of the product were extremely disappointed. We started to wonder what was happening across the San Francisco Bay at Sybase's Emeryville headquarters. Meanwhile, our relationship with and respect for Oracle was quite different.

## AN HONORABLE FIGHT AGAINST ORACLE

Up to this point, the fight between Informix and Oracle had been polite and chivalrous. Partly because both companies were so busy hammering away at Sybase, they hadn't had many direct confrontations. From Oracle's standpoint, the company hadn't had any reason to worry about Informix since we had been relegated to the low end of the database market. From our standpoint, we were on a crusade to defeat Sybase. It was very helpful to have Sybase fighting wars on two different fronts against Oracle and Informix.

The relationship between Larry Ellison and Phil White was similarly cordial and respectful. They attended many of the same speaking engagements, occasionally lunched at one of Phil's restaurants, and their children rode horses at the same stable on weekends. Phil would continually tell the press he wasn't in a fight with Larry Ellison: "Ellison wants to make more money than Bill Gates, for which he intends to challenge every one of the niches that exist in the market. We prefer to keep out of this fight, and focus ourselves on the technology aspect."[17]

For his part, Ellison even passed along compliments to Informix. For example, when Informix OnLine Dynamic Server was released, he said, "I have a lot of respect for what Informix has done with its core database technology."[18] Phil and Ellison, along with their CFOs, even met privately at Ellison's house to talk about the possibility of merging the two companies. Another well-publicized incident that helps explain the nature of their relationship was recounted in this *Computerweekly* excerpt.

> Having won a bet on a ball game they decided to celebrate in the restaurant part-owned by White. One of the party, according to at least one top Informix source, was a lovely and nubile young lass definitely likely to interest amorous Ellison. Fortunately, Ellison was forewarned that the siren was in fact Phil White's sister-in-law and to keep his intentions purely honourable. So honourable, apparently, that he was moved to exclaim, "Phil, if I married her we'd be brothers-in-law." Which brings to mind the old Machiavellian adage, "Keep your friends close, but your enemies closer."[19]

When later Informix rose to take the place of Sybase as Oracle's number one competitor, the fighting would take a very nasty turn. The upcoming battle would cause both companies to focus their strengths on their opponent's weaknesses. However, for now, one of Informix's past strengths was quickly becoming its Achilles heel.

## THE CHANGING LANDSCAPE OF APPLICATION DEVELOPMENT

Informix had historically derived nearly half of its revenue from application development tools: I-SQL, ESQL-C, and more importantly, Informix 4GL. However, all of these products were character based. They did not support a GUI (graphical user interface), which had become a customer requirement.

I-SQL was an ad hoc query tool that was also used for building rudimentary applications. Given the new generation of graphical tools, one frustrated developer referred to it as "a cassette powered typewriter."[20] On the other hand, Informix 4GL was a very powerful tool that was used to build mission-critical applications such as the Hyatt Hotels' reservation system. Hard-core C and COBOL programmers who liked to work directly with source code loved it. However, the new generation of Windows-based programmers would not even consider such a passé product.

A paradigm shift had occurred in how applications were-built. The new trend was "RAD," or rapid application development. RAD enabled a developer to build an application quickly by designing the user interface first and then inserting prebuilt objects that vendors included with their products. These tools offered visual programming environments in which the developer's screen was similar to a painter's canvas. They were easier to use than the current generation of tools and, equally important, worked with any database.

The Informix tools lacked "sex appeal" when compared to the three most prominent RAD development tools of the day: Powersoft's PowerBuilder, Microsoft's Visual Basic, and Gupta's SQLWindows. Overall, PowerBuilder was the tool of choice. Wherever the company held product demonstration seminars, the rooms would be packed with programmers eager to learn more. Industry magazines wrote about PowerBuilder extensively, and the want ads were filled with companies seeking anyone with PowerBuilder experience. Power-Builder was the hot product, and its salespeople naturally gravitated toward working with Sybase since Oracle and Informix always pushed their own tools on customers.

The only real alternative to PowerBuilder was Microsoft's Visual Basic. It became the natural desktop choice because it was thought that only Microsoft would keep up with its continuously changing Windows interface. A huge third-party market also existed for VBXs

(Visual Basic Extensions), including spreadsheets, editors, and graphs that made programming easier.

At Informix, we argued that if you were building an application that connects to only one vendor's database, you should use the tool that comes from the database company because future improvements to the database would be more quickly supported. In other words, the database and tool feature sets would always be in synch. However, in comparison to Oracle's tools, ours were not as exciting. Therefore, Informix had to win the database decision first. We couldn't lead or compete with our 4GL tools alone.

## MODERNIZING INFORMIX'S 4GL

Informix was late in trying to bring Informix 4GL into the graphical world. The first attempt was a product called "4GL/GX." While its intent was to make existing character-based 4GL applications graphical, it fell far short of its goal in the real world. The result was a product that didn't fully support the native Windows functionality, and the customer base rejected it. New customers who were also evaluating the other state-of-the-art tools were even more unimpressed.

After the failure of 4GL/GX, Informix launched a $20 million development effort to build a new object-oriented 4GL. Under the code name "4GL++" (named after the popular C++ object-oriented programming language), the product was promoted relentlessly internally, but its availability was continually delayed. As the product was about to be released, Phil changed its name to "NewEra." Most of the sales force hated this name because of the popular laundry detergent of the same name.

NewEra's initial product functionality was way behind that of the leading competitive product, the product was difficult to use, and it was way overpriced. We had to charge users for run-time licenses, when almost all other products did not charge run-time fees. Worse, third-party libraries and objects that speeded application development were not available as they were for Visual Basic and Power-Builder.

It was quickly obvious to the sales force that the product was not going to dominate Powersoft, Visual Basic, and Oracle's development tool called Oracle Forms the way the marketing and engineering folks had promised us. The misleading marketing hype caused the salespeople to pursue business we couldn't win. It damaged our credibility because customers quickly recognized the product's limitations. As a result, they discounted what we told them about our database.

When NewEra was finally introduced in the third quarter of 1994, it was too late. The tools market had matured, the leaders were set, and gaining a foothold in the client-server space would be nearly impossible. Within a few months of its release, Phil decided to deemphasize Informix's tools business. Marketing and development budgets were scaled back accordingly. This proved to be the right decision. By the end of the year, the rise of tools using Java and HTML (Hyper-Text Markup Language), the tools needed to develop Web sites, would change the application development tools market forever.

Even though most of the sales force was hoping for the acquisition of one of the other popular development tools, Phil wasn't interested. His position was, "The bloom is off the tools business. Today, most big customers buy packages. They buy a human resource package, they buy a manufacturing package, they buy an accounting package. The biggest software companies have their own tools: SAP has Abap, PeopleSoft has PeopleTools."[21] Conversely, he argued that the PC-based market would be dominated by Microsoft products such as Visual Basic, which was basically free.

The failure of NewEra wasn't a total surprise. We were UNIX server experts who simply didn't understand Windows desktop development. In fact, every new product that we tried to develop outside of UNIX was far from a success. Products on this list included OnLine for Novell Netware, Microsoft NT, and DEC VMS; mainframe connectivity products Informix DRDA and Enterprise Gateway, and desktop products Wingz, Hyperscript, ViewPoint, and NewEra. When the company strayed out of its UNIX server "sweet spot," it was almost certain to fail. Meanwhile, Sybase was about to defocus itself with a major acquisition of Powersoft, the number one provider of application development tools.

## SYBASE MAKES ANOTHER MISTAKE

On the surface, the Sybase acquisition of Powersoft looked like a winner. Sybase had been the only major database company without quality application development tools. A natural synergy seemed to exist between the two companies as half of Powersoft's customers ran on Sybase. They had high hopes that the $943 million marriage, the second-largest software merger at that time, would level the playing field against Oracle.[22]

Predictably, once the merger was announced, the other database vendors immediately stopped working with Powersoft. "There's no way Oracle is going to help Sybase gain market share at the desktop," said a noted industry consultant.[23] Non-Sybase database customers also sensed Powersoft wouldn't fully support their databases. One customer was quoted as saying, "I didn't get the impression they were committed to Informix. We're extremely committed to Informix more so than to PowerBuilder."[24] No matter how hard it tried to fight the public impression that it was still open to all databases, PowerBuilder was immediately considered a proprietary tool.

PowerBuilder had gained popularity as a traditional "fat-client" development tool. It was considered "fat" because all of the application logic resided on the client's PC. However, the paradigm for developing applications was about to change radically. Soon, "thin" would be in. The Internet was completely changing the architecture of applications. The Internet required thin-client, browser-based applications that could be distributed in multiple tiers upon application servers. Both of these requirements were exactly opposite to Powersoft's strengths.

Three years after the fact, the Sybase-Powersoft merger was viewed with mixed opinions. "Sybase has lost focus as a database player," asserted Betsy Burton, a research director at the Gartner Group. "Its UNIX database revenue is eroding, but tools sales are growing stronger. Their major issue is choosing an identity as a database or tools provider."[25]

While the merger confused Sybase, it actually helped Informix. In the same way the Innovative merger caused internal battles within Informix, the Powersoft merger defocused Sybase from its core UNIX database market. Meanwhile at Informix, a development effort to completely rearchitect Informix OnLine, our flagship database, was nearing completion.

## A PORTLAND PROJECT SETS THE AGENDA OF THE DATABASE INDUSTRY

In 1991, a joint development project between Sequent Computers and Informix began that would set the agenda for the database industry for years. Oregon-based Sequent Computers was the leading manufacturer of symmetrical multiprocessing (SMP) computers for the UNIX marketplace at the time. Also known as "shared everything" systems, SMP systems are multiprocessor computers that typically have between two and sixteen CPUs sharing the operating system, memory, and disk storage. These systems are ideally suited for handling large applications because the processing load is shared among all the CPUs for optimum performance.

The joint project with Sequent resulted in an entire rearchitecting of the core of the Informix OnLine database specifically for the

SMP environment. The project was led by Informix's Gary Kelly, who hired many of the Sequent engineers (over the objections of Sequent's senior management) to finish the redesigned database. (Remember his name because he will be the center of a well-publicized lawsuit with Oracle later.)

The new SMP-enabled database was named "OnLine Dynamic Scaleable Architecture" and initially released as "OnLine Dynamic Server 7.0" (also known as "OnLine version 7.0"). OnLine 7.0 was years ahead of anything produced by Oracle and Sybase. The "dynamic" part of the architecture is what made it so powerful and appealing to customers. Processing was truly shared by virtual processes that migrated between the CPUs based upon load. The architecture meant OnLine could do everything that its predecessor could but faster and on larger amounts of data. Meanwhile, Oracle and Sybase either fixed their virtual processes to a particular CPU or relied on one virtual process to act as the task manager for all the others. The problem with either of these architectures is that performance degraded as the loads increased.

For the sales force, presenting OnLine Dynamic Server to customers was actually fun. Customers quickly understood the competitors' limitations. In the instances where our product wasn't selected, both the customer and the Informix salesperson knew that it was a purely political decision based upon personal biases. Customers could not honestly claim the other databases were better. OnLine 7.0 had more advanced disk management capabilities and superior recovery features, and it was easier to set up and administer. OnLine 7.0 was a product designed with the customer in mind.

## LESSONS LEARNED FROM 1993–1994

While Sybase's merger mania caused it to ignore its customers, Informix was able to capture the hearts and minds of new customers with a single prevailing argument: speed. As Sybase changed its focus from UNIX servers to the desktop, Informix quietly designed and rearchitected its flagship UNIX database with the next-generation-customer requirements in mind.

"Always take the customer's point of view" happened to be one of Phil's favorite sayings. A plaque with this saying and Phil's engraved signature was displayed at most every sales office around the world. While the customer focus would pay handsome dividends for Informix in 1995, three key business and leadership lessons can be learned from the period of 1993~1994 at Informix.

- Speed rules. The number one enterprise technology requirement is performance. Superior features and functionality are meaningless when performance is questioned. Informix was able to win the tangible and philosophical performance arguments with verifiable benchmark results and architecture comparison presentations.

- Abandon confused and crowded markets. In a period of four years, the entire application development tools market changed. The coupling of the tools to the database separated with the advent of client-server. Application providers such as SAP, PeopleSoft, and Oracle used their own tools to build their solutions, locking out third-party toolmakers. Finally, the client-server paradigm transitioned from "fat" to "thin" clients in response to the growing popularity of the Internet. Launching a product into a tumultuous market segment such as tools was a certain loser.

- Know your sweet spots. Sybase's acquisitions of Gain and Powersoft defocused it from the UNIX database market. Meanwhile, Informix stayed focused on its archrival Sybase, coexisted with supersized Oracle, and released a completely rearchitected version of Informix OnLine.

*A few hours of mountain climbing can turn a villain and a saint into two rather equal creatures.*

FRIEDRICH NIETZSCHE

# 4

# Nothing but Databases

## 1995

*Lose sight, lose fight.*

U.S. AIR FORCE FIGHTER PILOT ADAGE

Informix was a company running like a well-oiled machine in 1995. The acceptance of our newly rewritten flagship database, Informix OnLine Dynamic Server, surprised everybody—Oracle, Sybase, and even ourselves. The year 1995 was to be the apex of Informix history, and the fiscal results taken from the company's annual report put its performance in context from an empirical perspective.

- Revenue rose to $708 million, a 51 percent growth over 1994 revenues of $468 million.

- Earnings grew 59 percent to $105 million.

- Informix's operating margin (earnings before interest and taxes divided by revenues) was one of the highest in the software industry at 22 percent.

- Days sales outstanding in accounts receivable, an indicator of whether customers are happy with their software, fell to 76 days in 1995 versus 79 days in 1994.

- Informix generated $66 million in cash and finished the year with $262 million in cash and cash equivalent investments.

- Revenue per employee, perhaps the most important internal measure of the company's human capital management effectiveness, was $270,000 per employee compared to $185,000 in 1990.

- Since 1990, Informix's stock had risen 3,400 percent compared to Oracle's at 987 percent.[1]

Informix's good fortune was also the result of good timing. The year 1995 is remembered by many within the software industry as one of the "golden years." Windows 95 had just been released, causing a surge in desktop spending. Customer budgets for client-server purchases grew by 70 percent as more companies moved their legacy applications to UNIX or bought completely new applications from PeopleSoft, Baan, and SAP. Demand was increasing for "browsers" to view data over the Internet as well as for programs and databases to deliver the information. *BusinessWeek* magazine called the software industry at the time "A money machine that's firing on all fronts."[2]

These were heady days for the software industry in general and Informix in particular. No warning signs gave anyone any reason to believe that two perfect storms were slowly approaching. The first one would hit Informix in 1997 and leave the company in ruins. The eye of the second storm would pass directly over Silicon Valley and level the entire software industry in 1999. Back in 1995, it seemed the golden years would last forever and the greatest days still lay ahead.

## GOOD TO GREAT

Jim Collins's best-selling business book *Good to Great* explains the differences between mediocre companies and great companies. One of the book's principles was the cornerstone of Informix's success: "Good-to-great companies did not focus principally on what to do to become great; they focused equally on what not to do and what to stop doing."[3] While Informix's success was due to our focus on relational database technology for the UNIX marketplace, it could be argued that its success was also the result of a company that stayed out of trouble. In the simplest terms, Informix didn't jeopardize its future with unnecessary mistakes, and when mistakes were made, the company quickly reacted and reoriented itself.

The Informix "hall monitor" was Phil White. He was the authority figure who kept people in line and projects on track. Even when he wasn't physically present at meetings, his presence was felt. "What would Phil think about this?" was always in the back of the participants' minds. It was a legitimate question since Phil was the ultimate decision maker and the final approver of every issue of importance.

There's an art to knowing what not to do, and one key Informix principle was that the company didn't compete with its partners, or VARs (value-added resellers). Phil described the Informix partner philosophy in a *VARBusiness* magazine interview: "I want our channel to view us as a technology partner in a long-term sense and not view us as a technology partner and competitor in the same breadth. I think 'co-opetition' doesn't work. You cannot cooperate and compete. Our goal is to build a relationship and let the VAR grow their business without fear of us competing with them. Oracle offers competition. That gives us a differentiator."[4]

What the CEO says in his corner office can oftentimes be totally disconnected from the sales force's actions in the field. However, this was not the case at Informix. The sales compensation plan was congruent with the policies of encouraging partnerships. Salespeople were paid fairly regardless of how the products were sold. This was in direct contrast to the policies at Oracle and Sybase. Their sales forces were motivated to take the business directly and bypass the partners. "We pay our sales force to help them [VARs] sell. Whether the product came through the VAR or through our sales organization, our folks get paid the same," Phil said later.[5]

The Informix partner marketing programs were well developed and generous. The application provider's sales force had access to the same sales information, product literature, marketing collateral, and software evaluation copies as did Informix salespeople. From a technical perspective, partners could tap into the same information sources as internal personnel. Application providers received internal copies of Informix Software at 10 percent of cost, and margins on the software they sold ranged from 25 to 50 percent, depending on the sales volume milestone achieved. Whenever Informix issued a press release, it almost always included a quote from a business partner.

Partnering was a core business principle at Informix, and the software industry recognized it. The partner catalog contained over 3,000 solutions in 1995, more than Sybase's and comparable to Oracle's. Partners played a key role in increasing Informix's market share. According to Phil, "We are outstripping Ingres and Sybase and gaining more share than Oracle. The thing that is helping us is all these applications that are rolling out. People are buying applications fast."[6]

A problem area for Informix had been Windows-based development tools. When the company finally released NewEra way behind schedule, the competitive products were well established and light years ahead in terms of functionality. "The company was late to provide tools based on graphical user interfaces. This allowed companies like Powersoft and Gupta to pick up Informix's business in application development tools," according to an *InformationWeek* article.[7]

In hindsight, it is easy today to say that building NewEra was a mistake. However, Informix 4GL had been a very popular tool for building mission-critical character-based applications. It was thought that this experience would result in a very robust Windows product, but this was not to be the case. After the product was launched and it was realized how far off the mark NewEra truly was in meeting the needs of Windows-based developers, product spending was cut back in spite of the project team's requests for more resources. Within the sales organization, the product was deemphasized and rarely discussed during customer presentations.

Another area Informix didn't venture into was acquisitions. Phil didn't believe in them. In another interview he said, "I think we are the only company that hasn't bought anything. We have a great stock price and a wealth of cash."[8] Commenting about Sybase's string of acquisitions and the problems they created, he added, "I think it is difficult to acquire seven different software companies and integrate, support and migrate without having some problems. Had Sybase had to do again today [purchase Powersoft], I think they would never buy them. Powersoft is about worth half of what they paid for it. I think the market has changed."[9] However, Phil believed wholeheartedly in one area, much to the chagrin of many at Informix.

## PHIL'S PINK ELEPHANT: SMART CARDS

Over the years, Larry Ellison promoted many pet projects that were near and dear to his heart. In 1994, he promised that Oracle's video-on-demand would forever change how motion pictures would be viewed in the home. In 1995, he introduced NC, the Network Computer. NC was a stripped-down terminal sans operating system and with very little storage. Ellison prophesied that NC would forever change the way people accessed the Internet. Conversely, Phil argued that NC actually stood for "No chance."[10]

Ever the unapologetic showman, Ellison even appeared on Oprah Winfrey's television show in 1996 for a special program on America's most eligible bachelor. Meanwhile, Phil was a practical and down-to-earth person. Comparing Larry Ellison to Phil White was like comparing flamboyant Cary Grant to straight-talking Gary Cooper. However, the one topic where Phil acted more like Ellison than his usual self was smart cards.

Slightly larger and thicker than a credit card, a smart card had its own microprocessor and memory. Phil proclaimed smart cards to be the successor to magnetic-strip credit and debit cards. He extolled their limitless usage: "The smart card, by the way, is, in my opinion, the next personal client. It is up to your imagination what you can do with this. We are going to get American Express to do away with travelers checks and go with this. We are going to get the Olympics to use this as a way to sign up for all the games you want to see."[11]

He personally recruited Hewlett-Packard and Gemplus to form the Imagine Card alliance. The alliance was to provide Gemplus card technology and Informix database software with HP's server technology. "I think we can start doing smart cards next year," he promised.[12]

Phil carried a smart card in his wallet and eagerly showed it whether he was making a customer sales call or a presentation to one or one thousand people. While people always listened politely, the tepid reception made it obvious that smart cards were an idea way off in the future. In some cases, the smart card conversation would detract from Informix's credibility. However, no one had the heart (or the courage) to tell the emperor that he had no clothes.

The Imagine Card project never gained momentum or customer traction. History may ultimately prove Phil right about smart cards, but ten years later it still looks like smart card technology is an idea still way ahead of its time. However, Phil's dream of the smart card was a small problem compared to the trouble brewing at Sybase.

## A TWO-HORSE RACE AFTER SYBASE PULLS UP LAME

On April 15, 1995, Sybase announced what had been previously thought as unthinkable, a $17 million loss. While any quarterly loss is upsetting, the real heartache for Sybase was the unexpected drop in the sales of its flagship database, System 10. Mark Hoffman, Sybase's president, described the situation: "Maybe we were a little overconfident, we were thinking that we have issues but will achieve our expectations. Those 'issues' include the painful realization that potential customers have shunned System 10 in recent months."[13] For the most part, those losses were Informix's gains.

While one analyst called it "A major, major surprise,"[14] at Informix we had been expecting the news for months. Sybase was being outsold in competitive situations and was having a difficult time winning new business. The company was surviving by selling upgrades and additional licenses to its existing base of customers. Worse yet, Sybase was locked out of the application market space since its database didn't work with SAP or PeopleSoft. Because its database didn't support row-level locking, none of the application vendors could use it. An article from *Computerworld* described Sybase's quarterly miss and dilemma further:

> Problems porting to hot-selling client-server applications from PeopleSoft, Inc. and SAP AG to System 10 also ate into Sybase sales, the CEO said. After roughly a year's work by the two vendors, PeopleSoft's accounting packages are due to ship on System 10 this year. However, Sybase ports of SAP applications have been pushed off until next year, Hoffman said. SAP must wait for Sybase to support row-level locking in its database, and that is not expected until System 11, the follow-on database to System 10.[15]

It's a rare occasion when your archrival admits defeat, but that's exactly what Mark Hoffman did when he conceded, "System 10 performs well on multiprocessing hardware of up to four or six CPUs, but it buckles as more processors are added. We underestimated customers' desire for head room in their database."[16] Ken Goldman, Sybase's chief financial officer, added, "We probably didn't invest enough in our core database technology, and that will never, ever happen again."[17] With these admissions, Informix was now officially the only alternative to Oracle.

The mood at Informix was sheer exuberance. Sybase was defeated! It was the culmination of a four-year war. That April day marked the company's capitulation. Just as an opposing army lays down its arms when it surrenders, Sybase salespeople left the company in droves during the following weeks while their Informix counterparts watched with an element of disbelief. After the mass exodus, Sybase chief operating officer Dave Peterschmidt said of the replacements, "It would take three to four quarters for sales personnel to come up to speed."[18] However, three quarters in the high-technology industry is an eternity, and Sybase didn't have the luxury of time. "When you're trailing, the last thing you want to do is take a year off and re-architect the sales force," said Ray Lane, Oracle's president.[19]

Many of the Sybase salespeople left for Oracle, the company from which they had originally come. It was rumored that one Sybase sales manager who went on to Oracle continued to sit in on Sybase's forecast conference calls, learning valuable information about all of Sybase's deals, until his spying was discovered. However, only a handful of Sybase salespeople would be accepted at Informix. There was so much bad blood between the two companies that we didn't want the bastards around.

The unexpected loss was the first for Sybase since its IPO, and Wall Street punished the company harshly. Its market valuation was cut in half overnight. Within days, a half-dozen class-action lawsuits were filed, accusing the senior management team of defrauding investors by continually ignoring the complaints of customers.

To survive, Sybase would have to reinvent itself. By the end of the year, the company had reorganized to include a conglomeration of information technology products targeted at disparate categories: a commercial database (System 10), application development tools (as the result of the Powersoft acquisition), a low-end database (from the Watcom SQL acquisition), middleware and legacy systems connectivity, and consulting services and systems integration. It wasn't one large company anymore but a number of smaller businesses under the Sybase name.

For the first time, Informix's market capitalization was twice that of Sybase's. Sybase's results would continue to disappoint, and in the second quarter of 1995 profits were down 58 percent on continually slowing sales.[20] Internally, Sybase was in chaos. Based upon the customers we met with, its reputation was in tatters. The database industry was now down to a two-horse race—Oracle and Informix. Whereas Oracle was also a provider of applications, middleware, consulting, and tools, Informix was now the last true database company.

It would take two years for Sybase to correct System 10's performance problems and several more years before Sybase supported SAP or PeopleSoft. By then, the wave of business process reengineering that fueled the purchase of enterprise applications had passed. A year and a half after Sybase missed its number, Mitchell Kertzman, former Powersoft CEO and Mark Hoffman's successor at Sybase, was interviewed about row-level locking—the critical feature SAP and PeopleSoft required.

> The $25,000 question. Row-level locking, or more accurately a lack thereof, has been a thorn in Sybase. When? Kertzman jokingly answered, "I'm sorry, there must have been some interference on the phone! I couldn't hear your question. Next question, please!" He then went on to explain the immensity of the problem, "We currently have active development going on row-level locking. As you know, locking is so deeply ingrained in so many parts of the database, it's not something you add in lightly. It's something that's being worked on. We've got a new philosophy at Sybase. We talked about what Sybase learned from Powersoft; one thing Powersoft stopped doing a long time ago was making delivery-date promises until products were in beta, and that's where we are on this."[21]

In the history of the software industry, never has the lack of a single feature caused so much damage to a company.

## WHAT DO WE DO NOW?

After the euphoria over Sybase's misfortunes had died down, a "What do we do now?" uncertainty swept through Informix. It was obvious that the next battle would have to be fought directly against Oracle. However, if beating Sybase was like climbing Mount McKinley, then defeating Oracle would be like climbing Everest without oxygen. Frankly, not many Informix salespeople were truly excited about taking on Oracle head to head as they had been with Sybase. Whether they would publicly admit this was another matter altogether.

However, the jousting with Oracle had already begun. In late 1994, in a sneak attack, Informix had rented a billboard on Highway 101, the major freeway directly in front of Oracle's headquarters (Informix's worldwide headquarters was a fifteen-minute drive south on the highway). The first billboard message was an announcement for an Informix user conference. Following the conference, another ad was placed that touted Informix as "The best database on 101." Oracle employees would have had to drive to work with their eyes closed not to see it. At the time, there was much backslapping in the hallways of Informix that we had one-upped Larry Ellison and fired a warning shot across Oracle's bow. After Sybase had been conquered, the billboards became even more confrontational.

The "billboard wars," as they were known in Silicon Valley, would continue for three years until Informix's collapse in 1997. They were a frequent topic of media coverage in the local newspapers and industry magazines. It seemed the press was more interested in our billboards than our products, as reflected in a *BusinessWeek* article. "Phillip E. White, Informix' feisty CEO, says he's paying only $10,000 a month to tell 30 million drivers passing by Oracle each year that Informix has 'snuck up Oracle's technical tailpipe.' Plus, thanks to heavy traffic near Oracle headquarters and his sign, 'Oracle employees get a chance to sit and look at our little jabs,' he says."[22]

The press reported that the signs infuriated Ellison. Ellison even called Phil to complain directly. One billboard showed the inside of a car with the word "Oracle" in the rearview mirror and several dinosaurs walking toward Oracle's headquarters. The caption underneath read, "Warning: Dinosaurs crossing." The billboards also attacked Larry Ellison personally. In a reference to his affinity for the Japanese samurai culture, one billboard showed a samurai sword broken in two. On one half of the sword was written "Oracle." On the other half, "Late," in reference to the Oracle8 database, which was way behind its promised release date. The caption read, "Maybe the warrior needs a new blade."

The battle soon escalated into each company's advertising, and Oracle even parked a mobile billboard in front of Informix's headquarters. The billboard read, "Informix: The best database company on Highway 101? . . . As seen in snail systems."[23] This was a reference to a prominent Oracle advertising campaign that used snails to show the TPC benchmark results of Informix. By now, many at Informix wished the billboard wars had never started. It seemed we had awakened the eight-hundred-pound gorilla and it was coming directly at us. On top of this problem, our newly rebuilt OnLine Dynamic Server wasn't working precisely as we had advertised.

## INFORMIX'S DIRTY SECRET

Informix's OnLine Dynamic Server (OnLine 7.0) had enjoyed critical praise in the press. The elegance of its parallel processing had gained many new fans. Industry analysts touted its superiority to Oracle, and Informix was recognized as the technology leader. Prospective customers also quickly recognized the architectural differences, and sales of the new database skyrocketed. There was only one problem: it didn't work.

When the first OnLine 7.0 customers went live, it was like the introduction of OnLine 5.0 all over again. The product performed pitifully and was half as fast as the previous version. The sales force was immediately directed to keep pitching OnLine 7.0 to customers but to somehow find a way to install OnLine version 5.0, which by now was fully debugged. Customers who had upgraded were immediately instructed to go back to the earlier version.

Completely rewriting a database is an ambitious undertaking under any circumstances. Taking a newly minted product and putting it into mission-critical environments is a recipe for disaster. Early customers reported the database frequently crashed or would just hang, requiring the entire server to be shut down. Query results often came back with the wrong record of information. I remember one customer complaining to me, "It's as if this thing has a mind of its own."

Once again, the heroes of the day were the presales engineers. A handful of engineers saved Informix from almost-certain doom. The engineers literally camped out at these trouble sites. They worked around the clock and over weekends, installing patches on a trial-and-error basis and debugging problems on the phone with the database programmers in Oregon.

The situation was tense. Had the press found out the product didn't work, we would have suffered the same fate as Sybase when it released System 10. To the astonishment of everyone within Informix, the press didn't find out. Several months later, one senior executive staff member remarked to me that the cover-up should go down as "One of the biggest secrets in the history of the software industry." Conversely, a juggernaut called "SAP" was on the tip of everyone's tongue.

## SAP DRIVES INFORMIX TO NEW HEIGHTS

In 1995, business process reengineering (BPR), the streamlining of businesses to reduce expenses and increase profitability, was in full swing among Fortune 1000 companies. Massive projects were started by the world's largest companies to modernize business operations that hadn't been changed in decades. These big companies sought to do more with less, and "corporate downsizing" became the buzzword of the day.

To totally change how a company conducts business is expensive, and it was not uncommon for these projects to cost hundreds of millions of dollars. Behind each of these projects was one of the big consulting firms (KPMG, Ernst & Young, Arthur Anderson, or CSC Index). The firms were responsible for evaluating organizational effectiveness and presenting recommendations for improvement to senior management. BPR touched every aspect of a company, from manufacturing to accounting, staffing levels to computer systems. Perhaps the most common and significant recommendation from these studies was the need to implement new ERP (enterprise resource planning) systems software.

The vendor most often recommended was SAP (over Oracle, PeopleSoft, JD Edwards, and all the others). Of course, the big consulting firms would also recommend their experienced SAP consulting practice for the implementation of such a strategic and necessary undertaking.

Fortunately for Informix, SAP supported only three UNIX databases: Informix, Oracle, and seldom-used German-based Software AG. Even better, SAP employees hated Oracle with a passion because its number one competitor was Oracle's applications. The fighting between SAP and Oracle was intense, with hard feelings between the two sales forces. After all, it's troubling when your enemy profits from your hard-earned wins.

SAP helped Informix penetrate two markets where it had been unable to gain significant footholds: the Fortune 1000 and big consulting firms. While Informix had been successful at *departmental* applications at big companies, now it was being evaluated as the *companywide* standard. It was costly and inefficient for global companies to support a multitude of databases. They wanted to standardize on one and would execute "enterprise deals," multimillion-dollar licensing agreements, for database technology across the entire company. We weren't coexisting with Oracle as in the past; we were pushing it out of companies completely.

SAP accelerated the evolution of Informix from a departmental provider of databases to an enterprise provider of technology. It introduced the senior executives of the world's biggest IT organizations to Informix for the first time. Since these organizations had budgets in the hundreds of millions of dollars, they did not consider spending a few million on Informix to be a big deal (even though we did!).

Informix evolved into an enterprise deal–driven company. Enterprise deals became a common occurrence at Informix and played a key role in its attaining the 50 percent plus license growth that year. The only way to sustain our revenue growth would be to continue to win more and more enterprise deals in the future. In this high-growth period of IT spending, this didn't seem to be a problem. We had a plethora of enterprise deals to work on. However, if customer spending started to slow, there would be severe consequences (and there were).

SAP also introduced Informix to an entirely new set of partners: the big consulting firms. Oracle had developed deep relationships with these firms through years of partnering. The consulting firms had built consulting practices to deliver Oracle's applications. Conversely, Informix was relatively unknown. The new Informix and SAP installations would require KPMG, Ernst & Young, and Arthur Anderson to become familiar with and learn our technology.

## INFORMIX SUPERSTORES

Each of the big consulting firms had built SAP centers of expertise around the world, laboratory environments where prospective customers would go to understand and evaluate SAP's applications.

Customers would use these centers to benchmark and compare how SAP ran on the different hardware platforms when the software was configured for their particular environment. The centers also provided a place where accounting firms could showcase their SAP-specific implementation tools and technical expertise in order to win over prospective customers.

The power of these centers to persuade customers to buy was not lost on Phil. He soon announced an ambitious $150 million undertaking to build eighteen "Information Superstores" around the world. The superstores would serve as demonstration centers where potential customers could test-drive Informix's products in conjunction with partner solutions.

Informix's software and hardware partners were excited about installing their products in the superstores. Software from the leading third-party tools and application vendors was to be installed on a wide variety of computer hardware including Hewlett-Packard, IBM, NCR, Pyramid, Sequent, Silicon Graphics, Data General, and Sun. Mark Tolliver, vice president of market development for Sun, said, "Informix's Superstores will provide our mutual customers a 'real-world' environment in which they can implement a thin client model to give their users faster access to corporate data."[24] It was quite a departure from the days when Informix was relegated to the low end of the market and second-tier partners. All the partners wanted to leverage themselves and benefit from Informix's success.

## PHIL WHITE PROMOTED TO BUSINESS ICON

The success of Informix bode very well for Phil personally. At the beginning of 1995, he received *Financial World* magazine's "CEO of the Year" award for the second straight year. He had become one of the most powerful businessmen in Silicon Valley, and he was a sought-after public speaker who gave presentations at investment conferences, venture capital gatherings, and prominent business events.

Phil's popularity also stretched beyond the high-tech arena and into the general business community. His self-assured, middle-aged authority projected naturally through the camera. All the articles about Informix, whether they were in *Investor's Business Daily* or *Information-Week,* included his photo. He personified the media's expectations of a CEO. AT&T featured him as the centerpiece in full-page ads in the *Wall Street Journal, Time,* and *BusinessWeek.* On a trip to Australia he was surprised to see a forty-foot billboard of himself on a building.

He flew nearly half a million miles that year to attend speaking engagements all around the world. However, "glad-handing" customers was always his number one priority. Our sales force always knew his attendance could make or break deals. But, his widespread recognition and newfound celebrity status made his presence even more powerful. Customers loved him. "Every person we dealt with at Informix—all the way up the chain to Phil White—went out of their way to nurture a relationship with us," said a key decision maker for Sears, Roebuck and Company.[25] Because Larry Ellison didn't make as many sales calls, Phil gave Informix a unique advantage. Customers were impressed that such a powerful businessperson would take the time to meet them.

Above everything else, Phil was a closer. He attended every meeting with the intention of "doing a deal." He knew it was his responsibility to take advantage of his position to close the deal. This aggravated some salespeople because Phil would negotiate terms and pricing on the spot in the heat of the moment. The customer at a major bank where Phil had played a prominent role said, "We could have accomplished our project on Oracle or Informix. But Informix was very aggressive on pricing, and they clearly understood our business needs."[26] When a customer shook Phil's hand at the end of a meeting, we knew the deal was done.

The more seasoned senior salespeople would use Phil specifically to break logjams. They might be dealing with customers who would continue to say no until they met the ultimate Informix decision maker. Sometimes, the obstacles were within Informix, so salespeople would use Phil to bypass the bureaucracy of sales management that naturally occurs within large companies.

In one instance, Phil was brought in to meet with some customers regarding a million-dollar license purchase. After working on the account for more than a year, the salesperson knew the account inside out and knew exactly how much money the company had to spend. During the meeting, the customers explained to Phil and reiterated to Informix's sales management their budget constraints. After the customers left the meeting, a lively debate about pricing took place amongst the Informix attendees. The salesperson argued the merits of the deal against the disagreements of his sales management. After listening quietly, Phil interrupted and said the salesperson was right and told them to get the deal done. To Phil, getting the deal done was always the primary objective and his number one rule.

## PHIL WHITE BREAKS HIS OWN RULES

Unlike at Sybase, Oracle's revenue growth had occurred mainly without acquisitions. Oracle relied exclusively on internally developed products. After the Innovative merger debacle, Informix also shied away from acquisitions. However, Phil ended 1995 with a buying spree that surprised his employees, the industry, and most of all, Oracle.

The first acquisition was tactical. Informix purchased its Japanese distributor (the database sales group of technology conglomerate ASCII) for $46 million.[27] Essentially, Phil bought out its contract to sell Informix products. Phil mistakenly thought end-user enterprise deals would increase if Informix sold direct in Japan. However, the existing sales force was more adept at channel sales and not as adept at calling on senior executives in end-user accounts. On top of these organizational problems, Informix's products weren't fully localized to support the Kanji character set and lacked multibyte support. In the end, Informix gained little through the acquisition.

Informix's second acquisition was defensive. The data warehousing market was changing rapidly. As the decision support systems in the first wave grew larger and more complicated, they became difficult to maintain and performance suffered. Off-the-shelf relational technology is extremely efficient for accessing for large numbers of transactions involving very few records. However, data warehousing tends to be the exact opposite: a few transactions and a large number of records. To solve this processing problem requires relational online analytical processing, or ROLAP. ROLAP database servers analyze data extracted from relational databases.

To enhance its data warehousing offering to include ROLAP, Oracle purchased IRI Software's Express line of tools in June. To counter Oracle's move, Informix purchased ROLAP start-up software company Stanford Technology Group (STG) in October. While Oracle paid $100 million to purchase the ROLAP leader, Informix paid $16.5 million for STG.[28] A similar difference in magnitude existed between the products' features and functionality. Even though Informix could now say it offered a true solution for data warehousing, Oracle's was far superior. Later, in 1998, Informix would acquire Red Brick Software to once again try to address its data warehousing deficiencies.

The final acquisition was strategic. The incredible growth and momentum of the Internet had caught everyone by surprise. Microsoft was caught flatfooted without a browser, SAP scrambled to completely Web enable applications, and Oracle and Informix struggled to find a way to store complex data: the pictures, video, and unstructured content the Internet required. With high hopes, Informix announced in December that it had reached an agreement to acquire Illustra Software for $400 million. Illustra was to be the foundation of Informix's Internet strategy. The combination of Illustra's DataBlade technology and Informix OnLine would create a new database called Universal Server. Informix had high expectations that Universal Server would have universal appeal that would propel Informix past Oracle. The reality of the acquisition would be quite different.

## LESSONS LEARNED FROM 1995

The year 1995 is considered the apex of Informix by many longtime Informix employees. Employee morale was at its peak, partnerships with the preeminent technology companies of the day were in full swing, and technical differentiation between our database and Oracle's and Sybase's was never greater. Equally important, Informix had avoided making any serious mistakes. However, the year ended with several acquisitions that were made with the intention of winning the next battle but in reality would bring down the company. What are the key business and leadership lessons to be learned from Informix's apex year?

- Focus, focus, focus. Informix reaped the benefits of years of single-minded focus on the UNIX marketplace in 1995. Informix was the UNIX database company. This simple single message was easier to communicate to all critical audiences—customers, partners, the press, and analysts— and easier to ingrain in employees.

- As the leader of a company grows more powerful, the truth becomes less noticeable. With so many accolades and awards being heaped upon Phil White, no one had the confidence or the courage to tell him smart cards were a far-fetched fantasy and his year-end acquisitions might be a mistake.

- Most technology acquisitions are made at the wrong time for the wrong reasons. It's common knowledge that most high-tech acquisitions fail to live up to their promises. In fact, very few actually create any real value. They actually increase the potential for company failure. Informix's acquisition of Illustra would mark the end of Informix's incredible rise.

• Luck matters. While chance does favor preparation, sometimes you need a lucky streak. Sybase's self-inflicted problems were a windfall for Informix. The fact that OnLine version 7.0's initial shortcomings were never made public was another lucky break.

*Appearances often are deceiving.*

AESOP

# 5

# World War III

## 1996

*Nobody roots for Goliath.*

WILT CHAMBERLAIN

Battle-hardened Oracle had withstood frontal assaults from Ingres and Sybase and had vanquished both foes. Now it was Informix's turn to lay siege to Oracle. While the Informix billboards had been the equivalent of saber-rattling, the acquisition of object-relational database company Illustra was a Pearl Harbor–type sneak attack. Shortly after the merger was made public, the Informix billboard was changed to read, "You have just passed Oracle. So have we."

The acquisition garnered industrywide praise. Informix's vice president of marketing noted, "It's very rare to see this type of consensus from the analyst community. We think we have a 12 to 24 month lead over our competition."[1] Meanwhile, the press considered it a coup. A *San Francisco Chronicle* headline read, "Informix Beats Oracle to the Punch."[2] Another article explained how the acquisition would finally merge the worlds of visual and character-based data, "The new, object-relational technology will, for example, allow vehicle insurance companies to store not only textual data about their clients and claims, but also maps and photographs of accident sites so they can calculate accident hot-spots and adjust rates accordingly."[3]

Most of all, the press loved the fact that it had another full-blown war to report on. Challenging power and authority was the reporters' forte, and they relished the chance to take potshots at Goliath Oracle and its know-it-all billionaire leader. Their articles carried titles such as "Database War Declared,"[4] "Clash of the Database Titans,"[5] and "Can Informix 'DataBlades' Slay Oracle's Samurai CEO?"[6] As in the war between Sybase and Oracle, the press once again published tit-for-tat exchanges between the companies' leaders.

> Phil proclaimed the Illustra acquisition as "a chance to take market share from Oracle and, yes, a chance to become the biggest database company."[7]

> Larry Ellison, Oracle's controversial CEO, questioned the reality of merging the two products: "It's like trying to integrate a boat and a plane; there is no way in hell this can be done. It's a joke. It's absurd."[8]

> Phil defended the acquisition and shot back, "Larry Ellison says you can't put a boat and a plane together, but we had the best brains in the industry looking at it for a year before we went with Illustra."[9]

> Ellison refuted the idea: "They will never integrate Informix and Illustra. It's the stupidest thing I've ever heard."[10]

> One of Informix's senior managers took the offensive and said, "These are the sure signs of anxiety. From where he sits, perhaps it looks hard. We have the strongest software team in the industry."[11]

> Oracle's vice president of server marketing aimed his arguments directly at customers when he said, "We think Data-Blades are inherently unsafe. One DataBlade could crash your whole system."[12]

> "Customers have a choice: They can wait for 'Oracle Late' (version 8) or use our database,"[13] chided Informix's vice president of marketing.

"DataBlades are the perfect name for their product. After all, you shouldn't play with blades because they're unsafe,"[14] Oracle's vice president of server marketing quipped.

Phil brazenly predicted, "Informix will be the biggest database vendor in the world in five years and the preferred supplier for users of database technology."[15]

An Oracle spokesman tried to get in the last word when he said, "We were the first to come up with a universal server. Don't believe the marketing hype."[16]

Although within the confines of Informix it wasn't uncommon for Phil to rail against Oracle and belittle Larry Ellison, never before had he made such confrontational statements in public. It was quite a departure for the cool, level-headed leader and a move many Informix insiders considered ill-advised. Phil was picking a fight against a company with three times his company's market share and four times its revenue.

The war was more than two companies battling for customer mind share. It was a clash between two testosterone-laden CEOs. "It was a battle of egos between Phil White and Larry Ellison," an industry analyst later said.[17] Phil's pronouncements about overtaking Oracle were thought by most industry insiders to be wishful thinking and "pretty wildly ambitious."[18] In reality, Phil's public sparring with Ellison detracted from Informix's credibility. However, in Phil's mind Universal Server provided a real opportunity to dethrone Oracle.

## WHAT IS UNIVERSAL SERVER?

The relational data model excels at storing alphanumeric information. Numbers and letters are ideally suited to the rows and columns that compose a database. The rows correspond to records, and the columns can be thought of as attributes (fields in the record). For example, a customer record might include the attributes of customer number, name, address, and phone number. A database user executes a SQL call against one of the attributes in order to access the record. For example, the user searches for customer number "8675309" or all companies in the state of "California." Because all of the database vendors adhered to the ANSI SQL standard, SQL queries against Oracle would be basically the same as those against Informix (a productivity benefit for software programmers).

The majority of the world's business information was (and is today) stored in relational databases. However, the rise of the Internet in 1996 created changes in the types of data businesses needed to store. The World Wide Web required more than just characters and numbers. Web surfers wanted access to images, audio, video, documents, and three-dimensional spatial data.

The relational model was not designed to handle these complex data types, and these objects didn't readily fit the SQL standards of the time. To address this deficiency, the object-relational software market emerged. Illustra, founded by Michael Stonebraker, was one of the companies that targeted this marketplace. Stonebraker is recognized as a prominent Silicon Valley figure, and his scientific research at the University of California, Berkeley helped create the relational database industry. Based upon his work there, he founded Ingres in 1982. After Ingres was sold, he returned to Berkeley and began research in object-relational theory that ultimately resulted in the creation of Illustra.

Illustra's secret ingredient was called DataBlades, plug-in modules that provided the support for multimedia applications over the Internet. DataBlades are special types of searchable objects that reside in database tables. However, Illustra didn't plan to actually build the DataBlades. Its strategy was to open up the database architecture so that business partners and third parties could build them. Stonebraker further explained the DataBlade strategy in an interview with *DBMS Magazine*.

We will write as few DataBlades as possible. We'll find somebody else who has the technology that we need, and license
it. We have a Text DataBlade, we have an Image DataBlade,
we have a GIS/spatial DataBlade. We licensed the Text Data-
Blade and GIS DataBlade from other companies and con-
verted them to our DataBlade format. In effect, we are
licensing extensions from the application experts who, in
turn, get an alternate distribution channel. There will be
dozens, if not hundreds, of such extensions. We hope to have
a big catalog and act as a publisher of extensions. In a world
where there's a lot of blades that go into your razor, there's a
big aftermarket of sales possibilities for selling DataBlades.[19]

The first discussions between Illustra and Informix started about
a year before the actual acquisition. At that time, Phil made the decision to build object-relational extensions internally with Informix's
engineering team. When the project's progress was too slow, he went
back to Illustra for a more serious round of conversations.

On paper, Informix and Illustra had a lot of synergies. Informix's
partner-based philosophy was well suited to the DataBlade strategy,
Illustra's sales and marketing presence was infinitesimal compared to
Informix's, and both companies shared a similar disdain for Oracle.
Phil said about his decision to purchase Illustra, "I bought the company when I could get used to the idea of paying $400 million for a
$5 million turnover company. We now have two of the greatest data-
base architects in the world. Mike Saranga, who designed MVS and
DB2 when he was at IBM, and Michael Stonebraker, who designed
both Ingres and Illustra."[20]

However, the merger raised big questions. Was there really a market for object-relational? The previous year's worldwide sales total for
object database technology was less than $50 million. How would
Informix successfully merge one million lines of Informix source code
with half a million lines from Illustra? Since Illustra and all the other

object-relational vendors did not have fully defined ANSI SQL standards to base their products on, each had to implement its own proprietary extensions. Would customers want a proprietary product in a standards-based world?

Following the acquisition, Informix went on the offensive with a marketing campaign of a magnitude never before seen from the company. Aggressive promises were made about the availability of the merged product, which was now named "Universal Server." Coverage of Informix's Universal Server dominated industry news. Oracle was caught off guard and had to scramble to mount a credible response.

A few months after the media frenzy had subsided, a technology columnist predicted, "Call me a skeptic, but I would be surprised if Informix delivers on this one by the end of calendar 1996. If Informix can defy history by incorporating major technology through acquisition, it will have a winner."[21]

## WINNING A DIFFERENT BATTLE

Oracle found itself in a never-before-experienced position as both technical and marketing underdog to Informix. Informix's entirely rewritten OnLine version 7.0 relational technology was clearly superior to Oracle's version 7. Oracle's flagship database was now five years old and considered long in the tooth. Informix was quickly claiming the next wave of database technology, which many predicted would be even bigger than relational: the ability to store pictures, sounds, and video for the exploding Internet.

Compounding Oracle's dilemma, the Informix marketing promotion was taking hold and Oracle was at least a year away from its version of Universal Server, Oracle8. Oracle needed to buy some time to get Oracle8 out the door. Therefore, its marketing machine had to persuade customers that Informix's Universal Server was too risky and not ready for mainstream use. Prudent customers would wait for Oracle8, the bigger, better, and safer object-relational database.

Informix's trench war with Oracle would be very different from its guerilla campaign against Sybase. Informix initiated a full frontal assault, a direct attack on Oracle. However, Oracle was a ruthless competitor that was unafraid to use any weapon in its arsenal. The company immediately mobilized its marketing machine to spread doubt that Universal Server and DataBlades would ever be merged successfully. Oracle waged a campaign to spread fear that the resulting product would be incredibly slow and, more important to mission-critical customers, unreliable.

To counteract the DataBlade argument, Oracle hammered on the message that the surest way to corrupt important business information was with DataBlades, which were developed by third-party amateurs who hadn't a clue about database reliability. Speaking from the other side of its mouth, Oracle immediately announced its own Data Cartridges program and said that fifty software companies had agreed to provide these knockoff DataBlades.

From a sales standpoint, Oracle implemented a strategy to "cut off the oxygen"[22] from Informix with ultra-aggressive discounting in competitive accounts. It launched a "Where in the world is Phil White?" internal sales program to track Phil's every move. Wherever he made customer visits, Oracle salespeople would follow and try to buy the business back.

Oracle claimed it had coined the term "Universal Server" and sued Informix over its use. Although the lawsuit was ultimately settled without success, it sent a message to the marketplace that Oracle had been working on object-relational software far ahead of Informix. The suit showed that Oracle would use any means necessary to slow Informix down.

In another sign of exasperation over the delayed release of version 8, Oracle redefined version 7.3 as its "Universal Server" and released it, in the words of one reporter, "With a marketing hype rivaled only by Microsoft's Windows 95 launch."[23] However, the 7.3 release was actually a knee-jerk response to counteract Informix: "Many analysts believe that Oracle 7.3 was never meant to be the universal database and that Oracle was pressured into introducing a universal database by Informix's announcement."[24] Informix had indeed caught Oracle flatfooted, and Universal Server was a very sensitive topic in Ellison's office. "Oracle is embarrassed," said one analyst.[25]

Meanwhile, another software Goliath was gathering momentum with its new relational database. Both Oracle and Informix anxiously watched as Microsoft's SQL Server continued to gain popularity.

## A NEW RELATIONAL DATABASE PLAYER

Back in 1991, Microsoft and Sybase banded together to port Sybase's SQL Server version 4 UNIX engine to IBM's OS/2. When the partnership between IBM and Microsoft soured, the porting efforts were refocused on a new Microsoft operating system called Windows NT. However, Sybase was busily working on its new System 10 release at the time and lost interest in porting its old code stream to Windows NT. Therefore, the two companies agreed that Microsoft would work on the 4.2 release of SQL Server for Windows NT and that Sybase would port its new System 10 product to Windows NT later on.

Since its release in 1993, Windows NT had been gaining momentum in the marketplace as an alternative to UNIX work-group servers. Although UNIX still dominated the enterprise, many IT departments declared Microsoft their standard and migrated to NT by default. As a result, Microsoft's SQL Server gained initial acceptance, even though it was considered a far inferior product. The fact that it bore the Microsoft logo was enough to encourage its widespread adoption.

If database buyers were playing a word association game in 1996, they would most likely have said, "Informix-technology; Oracle-biggest; Sybase-risky; Microsoft-mediocre." The following user group posting sums up the state of the database market and the NT-versus-UNIX decision: "Well, choose a database first, and don't run on NT. NT is fine when it works automagically, but if things go wrong I'd rather support UNIX any day! I've worked with Oracle and Informix. I found Oracle really horrid: system admin was a confusing mess and the tools were appalling. I really enjoy working with Informix: it has great technology, outstanding performance and it's relatively fresh (having been rewritten)."[26]

In 1996, for the first time Windows NT actually outsold UNIX, 725,000 to 602,000 servers.[27] Even though most of the NT systems were low-end servers, it was obvious that NT would challenge UNIX and that Microsoft would soon refine SQL Server into a formidable product. Still, Informix paid very little attention to the burgeoning NT marketplace and had yet to ship a single piece of software for NT.[28] At the expense of an effort to create a robust database for Windows NT, the Illustra acquisition received all of the attention from the engineering, marketing, and sales departments at Informix. However, confusion was growing within the Informix sales force about what product to sell, OnLine Dynamic Server or Universal Server.

## WHAT DO WE SELL?

By the middle of the year, the Informix salespeople had a major problem—they believed the Universal Server marketing hype as much as everyone else. However, it wasn't the sales force's fault that Informix's marketing had run amok. In another sense, it wasn't marketing's fault either. Everyone had taken Phil's mandate to heart. We believed him when he said Universal Server was the company's future: "Today, we manage less than 20 percent of the data that a company uses day to day. With a relational-object environment, we can handle 100 percent of the data. Imagine if you have all the data that's stored in e-mails, voice mails, faxes, filing cabinets and current databases and made it accessible inside companies using a low-cost environment such as the Internet."[29]

Knowing what we know about the Internet today, we can see that Phil's grand vision was exactly right. However, like Roger Sippl's purchase of Innovative, the Illustra acquisition never achieved the company's lofty goal. It wasn't solely for lack of technical functionality. Rather, customers of the time weren't nearly as enthralled with the universal vision as Informix and Oracle were. In fact, Informix and Oracle were squabbling over a nonexistent market. Nearly a decade later, the enterprise-wide marriage of textual data to voice and graphics is still a fanciful dream to most companies.

The Informix salespeople had become fixated on the Universal Server message. For the first time in six years, Informix deviated from the focused sales theme of performance to a more nebulous theme of managing all of a company's information assets. Presenting Universal Server to companies so far ahead of its fourth-quarter availability date created its own series of problems, including frequent changes in information, misinformation, and genuine confusion about DataBlade availability and pricing and overall Universal Server functionality.

The chaos was compounded when a potential customer asked for an evaluation copy of the product. The sales strategy was to first install Illustra's database and then migrate the customer to Universal Server later on. Salespeople had to fill out a multitude of internal forms and somehow get one of the few Illustra consultants (the Informix technical engineers weren't yet trained on Illustra's software) on-site to try to get the persnickety software to work.

The ultimate shocker came when the sales force was told the company would soon announce that Informix OnLine, the heart and soul of the company's revenue stream, would be discontinued in an ultra-aggressive push to get all customers on Universal Server. "There's no reason to [ship Informix OnLine] after the third quarter [of 1997]," Informix's director of database marketing said in the press.[30] The sales force thought the announcement was sheer lunacy. Why would customers buy an obsolete product? How could anyone force thousands of customers who had implemented OnLine in their mission-critical environments to move to a new untested product in a few months? Given Informix's track record for releasing working databases on the first try, the announcement was totally inane.

When a skeptical interviewer asked Phil whether one database could support both online transaction processing applications and complex data, Phil somewhat prophetically replied, "The real issue is performance. Can we drive thousands of transactions per second with the Universal Server?"[31] When Universal Server was finally released at the end of the year, the answer to this question was an emphatic "No!" Universal Server did not perform well, nor did it scale under heavy loads of database queries.

Yet again, Informix had another performance crisis on its hands. However, this time the situation was different. The interoperation between Illustra and Informix had increased the complexity of the problem tenfold. Software patches and other quick fixes wouldn't solve the problem as they had in the past because serious architecture synchronization issues had to be solved. As obvious as Universal Server's performance problems were, the company was also facing a subtle but equally serious set of cultural challenges.

## INFORMIX CULTURE CHANGES

The four thousandth Informix employee hired was very different from the four hundredth. A big-company "nine to five" mentality had replaced the "get it done at any cost" attitude of the early days. Along with all the success the company had enjoyed came an attitude of entitlement. It seemed all the employees were now solely looking out for themselves. Instead of rallying together to solve problems as in the past, people sought to condemn and punish scapegoats. The fun of working for Informix was gone.

The company's formerly cost-conscious behavior had changed from lean and mean to one that was bloated and bureaucratic. In a very un-Informix-like decision, Phil decided to spend $62 million for property and a build-to-suit high-rise tower to serve as the new worldwide headquarters. In many ways, the new million-square-foot building represented the opposite of what had made Informix great.

Because Oracle's and Informix's headquarters were just minutes apart, customers would frequently visit both companies for corporate briefings on a single trip to Silicon Valley. Many customers remarked that they appreciated Informix's no-nonsense headquarters versus the glitz and glamour of Oracle's palatial complex. One customer echoed these sentiments when he said, "When we visited two sites, you could see immediately that Informix has a better plan for controlling costs. I could see that Informix is focused on spending its money on the area that matters most to its customers—research and development—rather than spending money on aesthetics."[32] Unfortunately, Informix had quickly turned into another Oracle.

The biggest cultural clash involved the former Illustra employees. To our astonishment, they acted as if they had bought Informix. They continually complained they weren't getting the attention and resources they rightly deserved. It seemed like the Innovative merger all over again.

Another change involved relationships. Through the years, partnering at Informix had been taken very seriously: we would work together with our partners to close business. Now partnering took on a fictitious and superfluous aspect. New partnerships were announced that astonished the sales force. For example, an announcement about a Netscape partnership caused complete confusion. No one in the sales force could decipher what it meant. Moreover, the lofty goals of new partnerships were well publicized but the sales force was not provided with anything to drive deals. As an example, an announcement about joint integration with Compuware was not followed up with any promotional programs or cross-training. It seemed as if Informix was now practicing partnership by press release, without R&D integration or the field programs necessary to create synergistic relationships.

An off-the-record change to the sales commission plan also greatly changed the concept of partnering. Historically, a salesperson was paid basically the same regardless of whether a customer purchased software through a partner or directly from the salesperson. However, for forecasting and commissions purposes, these two types of deals were placed into one of two categories: indirect (through a partner) or direct (from the salesperson).

While not an official policy, sales management was interested only in direct revenue. Only direct deals were discussed in forecast and sales meetings. The only time indirect business was talked about in detail was in strategy sessions to find a way to cut out partners and make deals directly. A salesperson who closed $5 million of direct business would earn a spot at Summit Club, whereas a salesperson who closed the same amount of business indirectly wouldn't. The insinuation was that direct business was "good" revenue and indirect was "bad."

Phil White had changed too. His trophy shelf was filled with recent awards, such as the Legend in Leadership Award from NASDAQ's Stock Market Center for Leadership, Entrepreneur of the Year from the San Francisco Bay Area Entrepreneur Awards, and Industry Executive of the Year from *Government Computer News.* Many believed that his laurels and press clippings had gone to his head. Cocooned by his lieutenants, he had grown uncharacteristically out of touch with the pulse of the company, its customers, and its salespeople. He wasn't as readily available for sales calls as in the past because his daily schedule was dominated by the Illustra merger and the failing Universal Server product.

## AN OMINOUS SIGN

As the year closed, many longtime employees felt they didn't belong at Informix anymore. After many years as part of a cohesive team, respected employees and managers began to leave. Gary Kelly, the Informix vice president of product development who had led the Portland rewrite of OnLine Dynamic Server, discreetly began contacting companies regarding his team's desire to jump ship. Unbeknownst to the rest of the company, eleven of Informix's top engineers would defect to Oracle the following January in what would become one of the most publicized events of the year.

Within Informix, the team of engineers had been lauded as heroes, and their forsaking of Informix sent shockwaves throughout the company. Informix immediately sued each of the employees and Oracle over the mass hiring. A livid Phil White even drove to Larry Ellison's house to confront Ellison face to face, but he was out of town. Phil took to the press, where he called Oracle "sleazy" and vowed to fight in court to the end.[33] However, the damage to the Informix psyche already had been inflicted. To add insult to injury, Oracle rented its own billboard on Highway 101 that read,

Informix: Hiring lawyers experienced in suing programmers.
Oracle: Hiring experienced programmers.
*"A public service from Oracle Corporation."*[34]

## LESSONS LEARNED FROM 1996

To an outside observer, the skies still looked bright and sunny at Informix. As the year ended, no outward indications hinted that Informix had major problems. Informix would close the fourth quarter with $270.8 million in sales, its largest quarter ever. It was the calm before the storm, and in ninety days the company would be changed forever. The business and leadership lessons from 1996 could easily be applied to every technology company today.

- Short-term victories can easily lead to long-term defeats. Wars are fought over the long term. It takes more than a couple of quarters to win a war; it takes years.

- Even the greatest leaders are nowhere near as great as their laurels and press clippings make them seem. Once arrogance sets in, the truth is obscured, judgment is clouded, and greatness is lost.

- The quickest way to ruin a great business is through a major acquisition. Phil thought Illustra would open up an entirely new product category, when it was actually a point solution that should have been part of the product line.

- Partnerships are not based upon press releases. At the heart of true partnerships are cooperative development, field sales programs, and synergistic views of the marketplace and customers.

*War may sometimes be a necessary evil, but no matter how necessary, it is always evil, never good.*

JIMMY CARTER

# 6

# A Terrible Year

## 1997

*A victory is twice itself when the achiever brings home full numbers.*

WILLIAM SHAKESPEARE

The profession of sports has many incredible winning streaks. Cal Ripken played in 2,632 straight professional baseball games, heavyweight champion Rocky Marciano put away 49 straight opponents and retired unbeaten, and hurdler Edwin Moses won 107 straight 400-meter-finals over a ten-year period.

Informix was having its own incredible streak going into the first quarter of 1997. Informix had not missed its number in seven years—twenty-eight straight quarters! However, that streak came to an end in the first quarter of 1997 in the most spectacular way. Informix missed its number by nearly $100 million. The company posted $133.7 million in sales, compared to $204 million from the same quarter a year earlier.[1]

The event was the catalyst for a series of remarkable events that would lead to a revenue restatement, class-action lawsuits, and the ousting of Phil White after eight years as its leader. Informix would never be the same company, and the miss marked the beginning of a "terrible year," as described in the introduction of the 1997 annual report.

To Our Shareholders:

Fiscal year 1997 was a terrible year for Informix Corporation. Our financial results were unacceptable and reflected the discovery of serious problems in internal accounting controls and business management. These results led to a restatement of the Company's financial statements, a major restructuring, and broad changes in executive management. There is no doubt that this situation raised serious questions among our customers, prospects, partners, employees, and stockholders about continued viability and ability to sell products to new and existing customers.[2]

The miss had been a complete surprise to the financial community. After the announcement, the market valuation of the company fell 45 percent in the next two days of stock trading. One Morgan Stanley Dean Witter analyst said, "Informix has a record for how quickly a company can go from being a factor to being fiction in investors' minds."[3] The miss also surprised Phil, and he described it as a "painful wake-up call."[4] He honestly hadn't seen it coming and had even told his executive staff members in the final days of the quarter that he thought they would make the number.

As at most other software companies, Informix's revenue was heavily skewed toward the end of the quarter. Up to two-thirds of the company's business came in the last few weeks of a quarter. This created a forecasting nightmare at all levels of the company. Customers had been conditioned by the entire high-tech industry to wait until the last possible moment to buy in order to get the best deal.

The miss wasn't a surprise to everybody. Many Informix oldtimers had been quietly predicting a meltdown of one sort or another. The company had been resting on its laurels and had forgotten what had made it great. Now there was some painful medicine to be doled out because the company would have to take drastic corrective measures.

## THE RESULTS OF THE MISS

Since $100 million in cash wouldn't be coming in, cash instantly went from a commodity to a precious resource. Layoffs occurred immediately, and the new worldwide headquarters buildings were put up for sale before the company even had the chance to move in. In light of the internal emergency, Informix dropped the lawsuit against Oracle regarding the Portland programmers because winning it wasn't important anymore. By coincidence, it was during this trial that Phil White first met John Keker, the lawyer who represented Oracle. Phil would later hire Keker as his defense lawyer.

In the weeks following the revenue announcement, dozens of class-action lawsuits were filed by lawyers on behalf of disgruntled shareholders who saw their Informix investments cut in half. Another unwritten formula in high-technology goes something like this:

Quarterly Revenue Surprise + Officers' Sold Stock + Lawyers = Class-Action Lawsuits

From the dozens of class-action lawsuits, the most prominent law firm to sue Informix was Milberg Weiss Bershad Hynes & Lerach. Milberg Weiss is widely acknowledged as the shareholder class-action lawsuit leader. It is also one of the most feared law firms in the nation. Since Milberg Weiss represented Informix shareholders who had incurred the most losses, all of the individual class-action lawsuits were rolled into one action under the firm's lead.

The *Wall Street Journal* made these comments about the lead attorney in the Informix case, William Lerach of Milberg Weiss: "Both Mr. Lerach and his firm are highly controversial for their lawsuits; critics say the actions are filed any time a stock drops, even when there is no fraud."[5]

A *Forbes* article said, "Weiss and Lerach fancy themselves as the number one enemy of corporate crooks, the champion of the small investor. But some Milberg Weiss cases paint a picture of a firm that abuses its power, pursues vendettas, conspires with short-sellers and buys influence among Democratic politicians. The firm is so pugnacious that even the most powerful chief executives are loath to criticize Milberg publicly."[6]

Another outcome from the miss was that Informix started a search for a new president and CEO of Informix. While Phil would remain as chairman, fresh leadership was needed to regain corporate credibility. As one analyst said, "At this stage, the only thing that counts is what sort of Marshall Plan the new CEO can orchestrate and how quickly he can implement it. He has to get up the learning curve fast, reduce headcount while retaining superstars, plug the cash flow drain, and put some controls in place. The toughest of tasks will be keeping the good people since the demand for talent at emerging companies in the Bay Area is insatiable."[7]

As expected, a mass exodus of employees occurred. The job market was red hot with exciting new firms addressing the Internet. After watching what Sybase employees went through when they hit hard times, Informix employees had little hope that Informix would turn around in the short term. Their faith in the company's future was gone, and their belief in its leadership had disappeared overnight.

## WHY INFORMIX MISSED THE NUMBER

"I feel terrible about it. I feel like I disappointed employees, customers, friends, and family," a shaken Phil White was quoted as saying immediately following the miss.[8] The initial Informix public reaction was to blame the shortfall on an overemphasis of Universal Server by the sales organization.

While Phil blamed the loss on Informix's misguided sales force, the real problem was the one explained in Geoffrey Moore's landmark book, *Inside the Tornado.* He describes a "tornado" as "a period of mass-market adoption, when the general marketplace switches over to a new infrastructure paradigm."[9] One of the fundamental rules for companies enjoying the hypergrowth of a tornado is not to introduce discontinuity but rather to stick with whatever product architecture they took into the tornado. Clearly, the mass migration to relational databases on UNIX was one of the greatest high-technology tornados ever. Informix mistakenly introduced Universal Server as the tornado started to slow, when it should have stayed with mainstream Informix OnLine technology instead.

Although the Universal Server overemphasis was perhaps the most damaging of Informix's many self-inflicted wounds, it wasn't the sole cause of the miss. In the end, the shortfall was the result of a combination of many different factors, including the following.

- Informix counted on big deals. Over time the company had moved away from bread-and-butter deals in small and medium-sized companies and concentrated on big deals every quarter. These big deals were all based upon pool-of-funds agreements. Whether they were executed with end users or partners, the effect was the same: they pulled future streams of revenue forward. Therefore, Informix needed an endless supply of big deals to maintain revenue growth rates.

- Informix tried a frontal assault against a bigger and better-entrenched competitor. Informix deviated from being the nicer, partner-based company and challenged Oracle to a fistfight. In one sense, Informix became another Oracle in order to fight Oracle. However, this strategy was exactly the opposite of what had made the company successful in the past.

- Universal Server was not ready for prime time. It performed poorly, wasn't well integrated, and didn't deliver on the immense promises that had been made in the press about it. The Internet was a completely new and unknown market at the time. Universal Server possibly could have influenced a new generation of database buyers if it had worked as promised, but only if it worked.

- Informix tried to sell an early-adopter product in a mainstream market. While early adopters are technology zealots, the conservative mainstream database marketplace was risk averse by nature. Informix customers using OnLine for data warehousing and mission-critical applications were not inclined to experiment with Universal Server's new object technology. The mainstream market adheres to standards. Customers and software partners weren't interested in learning or supporting proprietary Universal Server extensions.

- Informix lost its focus. Management was too busy with the politics surrounding the Illustra acquisition, the battle against Oracle, and the integration and promotion of Universal Server. The company took its eye off the core markets, online transaction-processing-based applications and data warehousing.

- Phil was out of touch. Managing a billion-dollar company is very different from running a hundred-million-dollar business. The company had grown too large to have a single person in total command and complete control. To compound the problem, his executive staff would not stand up against or challenge him. Instead, he was sequestered from the rest of the company by his handlers, and as a result, he lost the pulse of the business.

Immediately after the revenue restatement, the company was in chaos. Employees were in a state of shock, wondering what would happen next. A massive layoff was rumored, and little work was done as employees fretted about their futures. The atmosphere was filled with doom and gloom. The best days of Informix were in its past.

## HISTORY FOR ALL ETERNITY

More than six thousand Informix customers attended the annual user conference in July 1997. Between keynote speeches by Colin Powell and the creator of the Dilbert comic strip, Scott Adams, Phil introduced Bob Finocchio Jr. to attendees on July 22. The former 3Com executive would take over the roles of president and CEO. One week later, Phil would be asked to resign as chairman of the board after an internal audit revealed accounting irregularities. The reign of Phil White was over with a whimper, not with a bang.

One of Finocchio's first actions was to hire Jean-Yves Dexmier to fill the position of chief financial officer. On November 18, 1997, Finocchio and Dexmier announced that Informix would restate the previous three years of financial results because revenues had been overstated by $311 million.[10] The shocking news was carried on the front page of all the local newspapers, and it was the lead story on technology Web sites and in industry magazines around the world.

Nearly two years later, in May 1999, Informix announced that a settlement had been reached in the class-action lawsuit for the first-quarter revenue shortfall. The $142 million settlement was one of the largest shareholder settlements in Silicon Valley history. Finocchio said of the settlement, "This episode will be a part of our history for all eternity. We can move forward unencumbered and we can move forward with confidence."[11]

The magnitude of the restatement had most certainly influenced the settlement award. Under the agreement, Informix's auditors, Ernst & Young, paid $34 million, the majority of the cash portion of the settlement. Informix's two insurers paid a total of $13.8 million, while the company paid just $3.2 million in cash. However, the company contributed $91 million of newly minted stock, thereby diluting outstanding shares roughly 5 percent.[12] The *Wall Street Journal* reported on the settlement, "Mr. Finocchio praised the settlement, saying it removed a legal cloud from the company with a relatively small outlay of cash. Using newly issued stock to fund much of the settlement is unusual but not unprecedented. While slightly dilutive to current shareholders, the practice benefits everyone, Mr. Finocchio said, because it allows all parties to benefit as the company's shares rise."[13]

In one sense, the settlement was an Informix victory since the company parted with very little of its valuable cash. But the real victors were the class-action lawyers. Typically, around 25 percent of a settlement amount goes to the lawyers while the rest is portioned out to shareholders. The *Class Action Reporter* reported that Milberg Weiss and the other legal firms received $44 million in stock and cash of the $142 million settlement.[14]

This was not the only time Finocchio had been involved in a Milberg Weiss lawsuit. He had been named in a class-action lawsuit against 3Com. The lawsuit alleged that 3Com insiders made $59.3 million from illegal stock sales as 3Com's stock climbed to $78 per share in December 1996. The stock fell to $37 two months later based upon downward revenue forecasts.[15]

## REVENUE RECOGNITION POLICY BEFORE 1997 RESTATEMENT

Informix salespeople had been continually encouraged by sales management to focus on big deals. In fact, sales quotas dictated it because they had doubled from 1991 to 1997 and were now around $3 million. As the salespeople would say, "You need a lot of transactions and a few big pops" to make it to Summit Club. The only way to get the "big pops" was to sell volume agreements. Volume agreements encouraged customers to buy more software up-front in order to receive greater discounts.

The internal term for these volume agreements was "pool of funds." These pool-of-funds agreements were entered into with both end users and value-added resellers. The difference between these two types of customers was in how they deployed the software. End users would use the product solely for internal operations in their organization. For example, when the IT department of a Fortune 500 company signed a contract for a $500,000 pool of funds, it could use the Informix software only for its internal IT projects.

Resellers, on the other hand, would enter into a pool-of-funds agreement with the intent of reselling the Informix software to their customers for profit. Informix's resellers included both software and hardware companies. Some resellers would receive a "golden master" from Informix, and they would install and configure the software within their application or on their computer hardware. Others would require Informix to send them "shrink-wrap" software, and they passed on the responsibility of installation and configuration to their customer, the end user.

Our main goal as salespeople was to get as big a pool-of-funds deal as possible. First and foremost, we would make more commission, and this was the only way we could exceed our quota to earn bonuses and accelerated commission rates. Second, a big investment by the customer in our products kept the competition out of the account. It solidified the Informix-customer relationship into a marriage. We knew the customers would incur bugs, find product flaws, and endure technical support deficiencies while they used our products just as they would with any other complex software. With such a major investment in Informix, however, small problems would be ignored given the overall scope of the relationship. In contrast, customers who made small initial purchases, whether from Informix, Oracle, or Sybase, were free to switch vendors at the first sign of any trouble (and they did!).

Ideally, Informix salespeople wanted to collect a check up-front when a pool-of-funds agreement was signed. However, if the customer's credit warranted, payments could be extended over a twelve-month period (usually in four quarterly payments). This was a stringent policy, and the company rarely if ever entered pool-of-funds agreements with payment terms longer than a year. Also, salespeople received up-front commissions only on payments made within the first year, since this equated to the company's recognized sale. Therefore, multiyear pool-of-funds agreements almost never happened.

Since the pool-of-funds contract was irrevocable, it met the generally accepted accounting guidelines of revenue recognition, according to the SEC.

> Informix followed an accounting practice of recognizing revenue from a pool of funds contracts at the time it entered into such a contract if payment was due within twelve months from the contract's signing. This accounting practice affected Informix's financial statements, by allowing it to include in its revenue payments it anticipated it would receive from a pool of funds contract at the time the contract was signed, even if the payments were not actually made by the customer until a later financial reporting period. At the time, generally accepted accounting principles ("GAAP") provided that such anticipated payments could be recognized as revenue before they were received if the contract met certain strict requirements.
>
> These requirements were set forth in a standard known as the American Institute of Certified Public Accountants' Statement of Position 91-1, "Software Revenue Recognition" ("SOP 91-1"). Following the standards set forth in SOP 91-1, Informix could recognize future revenue from a pool of funds contract at the time the contract was signed if the following requirements, among others, were met: (a) Informix had delivered the software to the customer; (b) Informix had no continuing obligations under the contract; and (c) the customer's payment called for under the contract was fixed and collectibility of that payment was probable. Under SOP 91-1, a fee was presumed not to be fixed if payment was not due until more than twelve months after delivery.[16]

Pool-of-funds contracts played a significant role in the sales growth of Informix. They accelerated future revenues forward, gave the sales force an incentive to work on big deals, and locked customers into Informix's products for the long term. Another positive aspect of the pool-of-funds contracts was their impact on Informix's service revenues. Maintenance was typically not included in the pool-of-funds contracts. (They covered only software licenses.) Usually, maintenance was invoiced separately once a year as a percentage of the entire agreement amount. Therefore, maintenance revenue streams were larger than they would have been normally.

## THE REVENUE RESTATEMENT OF 1997: A MATTER OF REVENUE "TIMING"

On November 24, 1997, Bob Finocchio and Jean-Yves Dexmier held a conference call to announce the financial results for the third quarter and talk about the restatement in further detail. On the call were press, investors, analysts, employees, and the general public. In his introductory statements, Finocchio said of the restatement, "It was massive in scope, immense complexity and very comprehensive, incredibly thorough, it was very hard work. We did it, I believe we did it the right way."[17] Dexmier then gave an overview of the numbers involved, which have been summarized in table 4 below (in millions).

**Table 4.** Informix Revenue Restatement

|  | Before restatement | After restatement | Change |
|---|---|---|---|
| 1994 sales | $470.1 | $452.0 | $ 18.1 |
| 1995 sales | $714.2 | $632.8 | $ 81.4 |
| 1996 sales | $939.3 | $727.8 | $211.5 |
| Total | $2,123.6 | $1,812.6 | $311.0 |

The difference between the originally reported revenues and the restated revenues was $311 million. Was this all fraudulent business? The answer is surprising. The reality was that almost all of the revenue would be rebooked and counted again in following quarters. Dexmier said, "Fundamentally what happened is that the company recognized some transactions which had been recognized as revenue were not final."[18] He went on to explain the restatement further on the conference call below. (All quoted passages from the teleconference are reproduced exactly as they appear in the written transcript.)

> The transactions which have been restated are primarily transactions in pool of funds. I would describe the pool of funds as a concept equivalent of a volume purchase agreement in which clients enters with suppliers the concept of which being that you make a commitment up front to buy a certain amount of product for a supplier in exchange for a discounted price. In the case here of the company, the company created general pool of funds by using the concept of volume purchase agreements for software licenses where those commitments were made by resellers and not end-users.
>
> As the company was not able to assess transaction part by transaction the full appropriateness of its revenue recognition, the company made the decision to apply very conservatively to existing accounting policies and procedures and therefore to recognize revenue for reseller license revenues on shipment to end users than a commitment by reseller.[19]

In other words, the revenue restatement was the result of a conservative change of accounting practices, not the massive fraud that had been reported by the media. In total, more than 85 percent of the $311 million would be reapplied over time, quarter by quarter.

Here's a personal example from one of my sales that further explains the accounting change. In 1995, Informix negotiated and entered into a pool-of-funds agreement for $1.2 million with a company that developed software programming tools. The company wanted to use the Informix database within its application as the change repository. The database would be deeply embedded within the application, and in most cases, the customer never even knew it was there. The installation of the Informix database occurred automatically when the product was installed and the company provided first line of support contact of Informix to its customers. Once a year, we would send the company a separate invoice for direct-support charges. The maintenance revenue would then be recognized as revenue monthly on a prorated basis.

The company's sales organization was self-sufficient and did not want or require any support from Informix during the sales process. This software company paid us the entire $1.2 million up-front upon signing the contract. Under the old accounting practices, the entire $1.2 million was recognized as revenue upon contract signing and payment. Under the new, more conservative accounting practices, this deal was debooked and the revenue would be reapplied in equal quarterly amounts, even though the company had already collected the cash.

This was the same type of deal that was debooked and rebooked later. Just as Phil had made Informix's revenue recognition practices more conservative in 1991, history repeated itself and Finocchio made them even more conservative in 1997. Dexmier said that the changing policy was timing related and that "This has been the cause of the most important part of the restatement."[20]

Since the advent of the software industry, the Financial Accounting Standards Board (FASB) has struggled to define how revenue from intellectual property should be recognized. In the early 1980s it was perfectly acceptable to sign a five-year agreement with a customer and recognize the software and maintenance revenue upon signing. Through the years, the board continually refined its accounting guidelines. For example, the board later required maintenance revenue to be separated from license revenue and required consulting services revenue to be recognized as a sale only after it was delivered.

Informix Software had adhered to the generally accepted FASB accounting policies during Phil White's entire tenure. The massive fraud reported by the press simply didn't exist. Rather, the new management changed accounting policies. "Our new policy boils down to a simple rule: to recognize (revenue and profits) when the earnings process is complete and we have no further obligation to fulfill. That is, when the product is at the end user," Dexmier said.[21]

If the majority of the revenue restatement was related to timing, why did the SEC file a complaint and the Assistant United States Attorney press charges against Phil White? Where was the fraud? Chief financial officer Dexmier explained further on the conference call.

> The year 1996 is, as you know, the bulk of the restatement. Net revenues restated represents $211.5 million. There were 56 percent in Europe, 35 percent in the United States, 7 percent in Japan, and 2 percent in the rest of the world. You will find those revenues on the balance sheets as "net unearned revenues" for $152 million, "deferred maintenance" for $10.8 million is due to timing of revenue recognition.
>
> Most of the $211 million is due to timing of revenue recognition. Out of the $47 million reduction in accounts receivable, there are approximately $20 million of transactions which I would characterize as "non-recognizable transactions," primarily being that transactions coming from eastern Europe where the company did not have a guarantee such as irrevocable letters of credit from eastern countries as far as payment is concerned.[22]

In the end, the $311 million revenue restatement wasn't the result of some massive companywide fraud. It was the result of a change in accounting practices and recognizing revenue, either over the duration of the contract or when the reseller ships the product to the customer. To this day, the press and public believe $311 million of phony transactions occurred, when fraudulent transactions actually accounted for approximately 3 percent of annual revenues. The fraud that did occur happened primarily in eastern Europe, under the direction of a single individual, and in a single instance in Japan. This is the $20 million of revenue that Dexmier referred to as "non-recognizable transactions."

## PHONY EASTERN EUROPEAN TRANSACTIONS

After missing the first-quarter revenue number, Informix sent a sales audit team to Europe to investigate why revenue collections were slower than normal there. In particular, collections in the eastern European region, consisting of Germany, Poland, Russia, and other eastern-bloc countries, were suspiciously late. The region was headed by vice president Walter Königseder, a longtime employee of the company.

The audit team found six phony transactions, for a total of $25 million in overstated revenue, originating from Informix's eastern European offices. The Securities and Exchange Commission would file a civil complaint in 2002 and obtain a default judgment against Königseder in 2004. The SEC argued that he participated in these transactions and approved of the secret side letter agreements. One of these transactions would become important in the case against Phil White, as described by the SEC in its complaint:

> On December 31, 1996, Informix's Munich, Germany, office entered into a $6.4 million transaction with Hewlett-Packard (HP) relating for licenses HP hoped to sell to Deutsche Telecom (DT). At the same time, Informix's salesperson in Germany signed a secret "side agreement" giving HP the right to cancel the deal and get its money back if DT did not buy the

licenses. Although Informix booked the entirety of the $6.4 million as revenue, the side agreement precluded revenue recognition. In fact, HP exercised the side agreement and canceled the transaction in February 1997. White learned of the side agreement in July 1997, and failed to disclose its existence to the auditors.[23]

When Phil learned of the Hewlett-Packard side letter with Deutsche Telecom, the SEC argued, he concealed it from the company's finance department while he contacted key executives at Hewlett-Packard in attempts to have it rescinded.

At about the same time, Phil learned of another secret side agreement that had been executed in Japan with Fujitsu. When Phil found out about it, he flew to Japan to meet with senior Fujitsu executives and obtained a rescission letter. However, the SEC charged that Phil actually wrote a secret side letter himself in order to obtain the rescission. These two acts would ultimately become the basis for the government's prosecution of Phil White. Another area where the SEC alleged financial misdealings was in how the equipment for the Informix superstores was acquired and accounted for.

## INFORMIX SUPERSTORE BARTER DEALS

Barter deals were nothing new at Informix. A Dow Jones article stated, "Mr. White, a celebrated deal maker, has used a series of imaginative tactics to battle hyperaggressive Oracle. When Informix landed Hyatt Hotels Corp., for example, Mr. White says he pledged to hold regular company meetings with the hotel chain. He tries to favor the long-distance service of MCI Communications Corp., another key Informix customer. 'I've got a philosophy—I want to use the products of customers who use my products,' Mr. White says."[24]

This philosophy also extended to the computer equipment needed for the superstore initiative. However, the SEC argued that Informix improperly recognized revenue for barter transactions with hardware companies. Even though Informix always structured the software sales and hardware purchases as separate transactions with cash exchanged in accordance with GAAP (generally accepted accounting principles), the SEC claimed the transactions weren't recognizable since significant deliverables remained outstanding. As a result, the true revenue position of the self-proclaimed "fastest growing database company" was clouded. Court documents submitted by the SEC further explain the commission's arguments:

> During 1996, the Company employed a sales strategy whereby various OEMs were approached with the concept of forming a "partnership" in which the Company would buy computer hardware from the OEMs to be placed in the Superstores and then used in joint sales efforts by the Company and the OEM "partner." In return for the Company's hardware purchase commitments, the OEMs were asked to enter into software license purchase commitments of similar or greater magnitude.
>
> Many of the OEM partners lacked a sales force familiar with Company products and expected the Company's sales force to have a substantial involvement in the reselling effort. The expense of the Company's involvement in reselling the software for the OEM partners was indeterminable but substantial based on the Superstore program costs alone. To encourage its sales force to assist the OEMs, in late 1996, the Company began to offer higher commission rates if a sale was closed through an OEM partner rather than directly by the Company. In the first quarter of 1997, former management gave the sales force performance goals to obtain end-user

orders to be applied against the OEM partners' outstanding commitments.

Under GAAP, if "other vendor obligations remaining after delivery are significant, revenue should not be recognized, because the earnings process is not substantially completed." The Company, however, recognized revenue at the time the OEM partners agreed to the purchase commitments notwithstanding that the Company was obligated to pay the costs and expenses of establishing and operating the Super- stores and that the Company's sales force was to perform all, or a significant portion of, the future reselling efforts.[25]

While the SEC argued that all obligations had not yet been ful- filled with the superstore-related transactions, even this debooked revenue was later reapplied. While not admitting or denying any of the SEC's findings, Informix executed a settlement in April 2000. Informix agreed to an administrative order requiring it to stop any future violations of securities laws. The company was not ordered to pay any fines, and it didn't suffer any other penalties.

## WHY WOULD THE NEW MANAGEMENT RESTATE?

Conservative revenue recognition was a prudent business move in a slowing market. It appeared that management had other reasons for the restatement. The additional $50 million per quarter of revenue from the restatement plus the service revenue gave the new manage- ment a much-needed cushion and improved the likelihood of a suc- cessful turnaround.

Not only would the new management be considered heroes for turning around Informix, hefty personal windfalls could be made in the process. According to a CNET article, Finocchio was granted 1,500,000 options worth an estimated $10,200,000.[26] However, the only way to personally profit from these options was for the stock price to rise above the price at which the options were issued. According to Dexmier, one by-product of the restatement was the creation of tax credits that would reduce future taxes once profitability was achieved. Theoretically, this would drive the stock price up. Dexmier explained this further on the conference call.

> Now the question is suddenly, what is the future impact of the restatement, and what is going to happen in future periods as the company continues its way? Two things are going to happen. First of all, we are going to have flow back of those earned licenses revenues and additional deferred maintenance to income. The current rate which we seek quarter after quarter is in the range of $15 to $20 million per quarter. I would like to emphasize that although this revenue is always nice, this is what I would call noncash taxable income, which means that this is not going to have any impact on the cash flow of the company.
>
> The second impact of the restatement is that when the company is going to turn a profit, we will have a reduced tax rate because we now have a very significant tax asset on the balance sheet for $61.2 million, which is mostly sitting in our foreign subsidiaries in Europe. So what is going to happen is when we get profitable, we are going to use this tax credit to reduce our tax rate.[27]

Apparently, a new financial model based upon the decelerating growth of the database market was being implemented. As opposed to using exponential growth to attain profits, as Phil had done, it seemed that the company would instead create profitability through expense management and guaranteed topline revenues. When asked about the decelerating growth rate of the database market in general, Finocchio said on the conference call, "It's not 50 percent, it's not 40 percent, it's not 30 percent, it's much lower, but it's greater than zero."[28]

The database market tornado that had lasted for years was over, and a new business model was needed that took this into account.

While it was understood that the majority of the expense reduction would likely occur in sales, marketing, and general administration overhead, the restatement seemed to play a fundamental role in the success of the revenue side of the new business model. On the investor conference call, Dexmier further elaborated on the business model going forward:

> It is a very simple action. That is something I learned in the first course of finance at school. It is called revenue minus expense equals profit. If your revenue is higher than your expenses, usually you make a profit. So here is what we have done. The first thing is we are driving to have a stable and predictable service revenue flow. The company is about to enter $70 to $75 million of service revenue every quarter. The second piece is that we have a rollback of advances on unearned revenue per quarter as you have understood, $50 to $20 million every quarter. Now the third piece which is really going to make the revenue is the new license revenue.[29]

The services that Dexmier refers to are mainly customer maintenance renewal support agreements. These agreements are paid for annually and provide a very predictable revenue stream. Together, the three pieces of the new model were incoming revenue from services, revenue reapplied from the restatement, and new sales. Most impressively, the company was now guaranteed to show $500 million of revenues on service and restated revenue in the first year following the restatement.

However, the challenge was going to be generating new license revenue. That would prove to be the plan's failing. Informix had lost so much key sales talent, and customers were hesitant to purchase software from a vendor whose long-term viability was questionable. In addition, Finocchio shifted the sales organization's focus away from big deals and established a new "hardware-based" sales culture within the software company:

> I have directed our sales force not to go after so many home-run deals. I am not sure they are good for the company. I am not sure they are even good for customers because we end up mortgaging the future a bit too much and oftentimes it doesn't serve the customer's interest because when they really need support it's hard to find.
>
> So we are actually going after what I would call smaller deals and shorter time frames where we can do a better job working with the customers on their real needs and not . . . this is kind of what I was talking about, sort of moving out of a deal mentality.
>
> Most of my career I spent in hardware and I could never get people to buy five years worth of routers in advance. I'm not sure it makes sense to get them to buy five years just because I can do it on paper instead of actually building something.[30]

At this point, many of the remaining senior employees in sales, marketing, and development left the company. However, the software industry treated them with a skeptical eye. The bad press left the impression that Informix was full of renegade cowboys and shady criminals. In reality, the next generation of replacement hires would be much less talented because joining Informix was now considered a dead-end career move in a red-hot technology job market.

## INFORMIX RESTATES REVENUE AGAIN IN 1998

Within six months of making the first revenue restatement, embarrassingly, Informix would have to restate revenues again. Ernst & Young, Informix's auditors, would not relent to the company's requests to include a $6.2 million deal that had been counted in the company's quarterly revenue figures. The audit firm was replaced shortly thereafter. Finocchio explained the reasons behind the restatement in a shareholder letter:

> Informix announced a restatement of its financial results for the first quarter of fiscal year 1998, which resulted in a reduction of revenue of approximately $6.2 million and a break-even quarter rather than a quarter with a small profit which we previously reported.
>
> The transactions resulting in the approximately $6.2 million of revenue were real and of substance—our product was shipped and the Company had been paid—and therefore we believe the decision to restate was a very difficult accounting judgment call.[31]

The decision on when to recognize revenue can be tough. Phil was criticized for his aggressive practices that were based upon counting revenues as soon as products were sold to resellers or OEMs. Even though Finocchio instituted a more conservative revenue recognition policy, the intricacies and complexity that surround revenue recognition had forced the company to restate once again. In May 1997, one month after Informix had announced its first-quarter loss, CNET published an article about the nuances of revenue recognition:

> Bean counting is part art, part science. Accountants must select a policy that will do the job and not alienate Wall Street or investors. High-tech companies' strategies run the gamut from aggressive to conservative. Analysts say that waiting until products reach end users before tallying up revenues constitutes a conservative strategy. Informix is more aggressive, counting revenues as soon as the products or licenses are sold to resellers or OEMs (original equipment manufactur-

ers). Both bean-counting methods are acceptable under general accounting practices.[32]

While bean counting is part art and part science, politics and self-interest also play key roles when a company decides to switch revenue recognition methods.

## THE AFTERMATH

With just under two years as president and CEO of Informix, Finocchio stepped down and relinquished the roles to Dexmier in May 1999. While keeping the title of chairman, Finocchio planned to spend more time with his family and pursue his lifelong dream of climbing Mount Kilimanjaro, the highest point in Africa.

Finocchio was widely credited with restoring Informix's tattered credibility and putting the company back on track. Thanks in part to the restated revenue, Informix was able to achieve six consecutive quarters of profitability. However, Informix's stock languished. In an industry article, Finocchio said his only regret was not being able to increase the value of Informix's stock, which remained at about $7 throughout his tenure.[33]

SG Cowen & Company analyst Drew Brosseau said it bothered him that Finocchio wouldn't see the turnaround through. He commented, "He's sort of half-way there. If it were me and I were confident in the prospect I would want to take the glory."[34] Another analyst was unimpressed by the sudden leadership change and said Informix still had a steep mountain to climb. "Before I would invest in Informix, I'd buy another coffee shop on the Embarcadero. You don't buy a minor player in slow-growing technology industry."[35]

In March of 2000, Informix paid about $1 billion to purchase Massachusetts-based Ardent Software.[36] After the acquisition, with Informix's stock price down 59 percent from the beginning of the year, Dexmier was replaced by former Ardent president Peter Gynes in July. One month later, Gynes announced Informix would simplify its business and move operations to Massachusetts. The simplification involved firing 430 Menlo Park, California, workers.[37]

Thirteen months later, with former Ardent Software high command now at the helm of Informix, all of Informix's primary database software assets were sold to IBM for $1 billion in cash.[38] The company retained all of the Ardent data integration products and business operations, and renamed itself "Ascential." Peter Gynes said of Ascential following the divesture, "Today we are focused totally and exclusively on data integration, and we have the benefit of the $1 billion in cash on our balance sheet to invest in our growth."[39]

Ingres, Sybase, and Informix had all failed to defeat Oracle. Today it is IBM's turn to war against Oracle. After the Informix acquisition, Janet Perna, IBM's general manager of the Data Management Software group, said, "At the end of the day, the team that has the most of the best talent in the industry will win this war. We are fighting to win, playing for first place."[40] In the words of Steve Mills, head of IBM's Software Group, "We are Larry Ellison's worst nightmare and the nightmare just got worse."[41] Here's some advice for IBM: history repeats itself.

## A FEW WORDS FROM ORACLE AND SYBASE

Early in 1998, Sybase disclosed that it would have to restate $43 million of revenues for 1997 when it was discovered that the president of its Japanese subsidiary and four of his employees secretly made side agreements allowing customers to receive rebates or to return software.[42] The restatement that followed also resulted in shareholder lawsuits. Mitchell Kertzman, Sybase CEO, said at the time that the database software business had traditionally been "run more on testosterone than common sense."[43] History has proven his observation to be correct.

In an interview one year after the Informix restatement, Oracle president Ray Lane offered his perspective on the Informix situation and Phil White:

> Sybase had reported it slowed down in earnings two years ago, and there was a real opportunity there for Informix to prove to the world that was a two-horse race. Phil White, who is a marketing and sales guy, saw an opportunity. I'm not sure any of us would have made a decision differently than Phil White. Now I'm not saying we are Phil White, but the chance to trash Sybase and get it out of the equation and say, now it's a two horse race between Oracle and Informix— well, you probably would have gotten on that horse as well.
>
> Now, did he know he was misstating earnings? I think two years ago, he did not know it. Having run one of these businesses myself, I think you can kid yourself. You start for a couple of quarters not knowing it, then some problems start occurring and you say, "we really shouldn't recognize this deal." For a couple of quarters, White recognized deals he shouldn't have. Then he started cooking the books. And what happened is that in the end, everybody remembers "Phil White cooked the books and lied to the public."[44]

Although 1997 had been a terrible year for Phil White, he continued to do very well in the years immediately following his Informix defrocking. Through his vast personal network of friends and Informix relationships, he consulted with fledgling start-ups and served on the boards of several high-tech companies. He was well paid for his advice. He made millions from stock option proceeds at publish and subscribe provider Tibco alone. But Phil's legal troubles were just starting, and his reputation within Silicon Valley would soon turn from tainted to toxic.

## LESSONS LEARNED FROM 1997

The year 1997 was the beginning of the end for Informix. While Informix's downfall was caused by a myriad of self-inflicted wounds, one person can be held solely responsible—Phil White. Several business lessons and leadership lessons can be learned from Informix in 1997:

- Revenue solves everything. Had Informix not missed its first-quarter revenue number, the company and Phil White would have continued on uninterrupted. Without the concealing cloak of revenue, every bad decision comes to light, weaknesses are exposed, and political infighting is set loose to destroy a company.

- A company's big-deal addiction will ultimately end in great pain. During the time of a tornado (a period of rapid growth), focusing on big deals is perfectly appropriate. As purchasing decelerates, missing a quarter is just a matter of time for a sales organization that relies solely on big deals.

- What goes up must come down. Informix had met or exceeded the investment community's financial expectations for seven straight years before the streak ended cataclysmically. Companies go through cycles of boom and bust. Similarly, careers experience periods of success and failure. Good times don't last forever.

*These are the six ways of courting defeat—neglect to estimate the enemy's strength; want of authority; defective training; unjustifiable anger; nonobservance of discipline; failure to use picked men—all of which must be carefully noted by the general who has attained a responsible post.*

SUN TZU

# 7

# The Wheels of Justice

## 1998–2004

*The devil is in the details.*

ANONYMOUS

In November 2002, more than five years after he left Informix, a federal grand jury returned an eight-count indictment against Phil White. Count one charged him with securities fraud violation, counts two and three charged him with falsification of accounting records, count four charged him with lying to the auditors, counts five through seven charged him with mail and wire fraud, and count eight charged him with knowingly and willfully making false material statements in a registration statement filed with the SEC.

Stories about Informix and Phil White's legal troubles were ongoing front-page news in Silicon Valley and featured prominently in high-tech industry publications. The articles carried titles such as "Informix's Infamy"[1] and "Ex-Informix CEO Charged with Fraud: Accused of Concealing Scandal."[2] The articles expounded on how Phil had falsified financial statements, engaged in insider trading, and manipulated the company's sales. However, the truth is more complicated than the headlines. Understanding the charges against Phil requires some understanding of standard accounting practices.

## WHEN IS A SALE A SALE?

Under generally accepted accounting principles (GAAP), for a sale to be recognized as revenue it has to be final and irrevocable. In other words, the customers cannot return the product at their discretion nor can the vendor offer concessions that decrease the likelihood of monies being collected.

The side letters that came to light shortly after Phil signed Informix's 1996 10-K (annual report to shareholders) were executed only in Europe and Japan. None were found in the United States. These side agreements would have invalidated the sales under GAAP and caused a revenue restatement because the company had included the bogus deals in its previously released financial figures. Specifically, Informix had recognized the revenue from deals that included side agreements. Two of these side letters would become the basis of the SEC's civil case against Phil White. This excerpt from the Securities and Exchange Commission's complaint against Phillip E. White describes the side letters further.

> In 1996, Informix entered into a number of pool of funds contracts. In particular, Informix entered into two pool of funds agreements in 1996, one with a European subsidiary of a United States company, and one with a Japanese company. Both contracts contemplated that the companies would have the right to resell Informix's software for a period of time which continued into 1997, and the right to make payments under the contracts to Informix into 1997 as well. The pool of funds contract with the European subsidiary required that company to pay Informix approximately $6.4 million, $3.2 million payable by December 31, 1996, and $3.2 million payable by March 31, 1997. The contract with the Japanese company obligated that company to pay Informix approximately $4.7 million, payable as the

software was resold, but the total balance due to Informix by November 20, 1997.[3]

Although Phil had not participated in the original creation of the side letters, the SEC argued that he attempted to conceal them from Informix's accounting department and auditors after the fact. His main motive was to keep the company from having to restate revenues once again. Another restatement would have caused even more class-action lawsuits to be filed against Informix in addition to those filed because of the revenue miss in the first quarter of 1997.

In conjunction with the SEC complaint, a criminal investigation was launched by the FBI and the United States Attorney's Office, Northern District of California. On the surface, it seemed the government had a compelling case. Informix had restated its 1994, 1995, and 1996 revenues and profits because of accounting irregularities. Revenue for 1996 alone was reduced by $211 million, and a $97 million profit turned into a $73 million loss. In addition, Informix's auditors had discovered other discrepancies with previously booked revenue relating to the Informix superstore purchases.

The SEC's investigation continued until May 4, 2004, when the commission announced a settlement in the case against Phil White. The settlement did not include any penalties or fines or require Phil to return any of his ill-gotten gains from stock sales. Nor did it include a "D&O bar," which would have been expected. Such a bar would have precluded Phil from serving as a director or officer of a company. Basically, Phil signed a cease-and-desist order in which he promised that he would not violate securities laws in the future. Upon the signing of the settlement, the SEC issued the following press release.

> Phillip E. White, Former Informix Corporation Chairman, CEO, and President, Consents to Permanent Injunction Based on Charges of Fraud and Other Federal Securities Law Violations

> The Securities and Exchange Commission ("Commission")
> announced today that Phillip E. White ("White"), formerly
> President, Chief Executive Officer, and Chairman of the
> Board of Directors of Informix Corporation, consented to a
> final judgment permanently enjoining White from violating,
> or aiding and abetting violations of, Sections 10(b), 13(a),
> 13(b)(2)(A), and 13(b)(5) of the Securities Exchange Act of
> 1934 ("Exchange Act"); Exchange Act Rules 10b-5, 12b-20,
> 13a-1, 13b2-1, and 13b2-2; and Section 17(a) of the Secu-
> rities Act of 1933 ("Securities Act").[4]

While both Phil and his attorneys were happy to have the civil
case behind them, they were upset that the SEC would release a press
announcement that claimed the settlement to be a major victory.
"Why Mr. Cutler (Director, SEC Division of Enforcement) and his
subordinates felt it an appropriate use of the Government's resources
to paper and then publicize a settlement agreement which has no real
substance is beyond us," Phil's lawyers would later write the court.[5]
The settlement had been the least of all the possible penalties the SEC
could have enforced. Conversely, the United States Attorney's Office
sought far greater punishment in the criminal case.

## THE CHRONOLOGY OF THE CRIMINAL CASE

While the civil case was ending, the criminal case against Phil was
gaining newfound momentum. The key to the prosecution's case was
establishing that Phil hid an MOU (memorandum of understanding) from Informix's accounting department when he signed the SEC
documents. Specifically, he had signed an S-8 stock registration form
knowing full well that the company's financial position was incorrect. In court documents, the prosecution provided this chronology
of events in the case of *United States of America versus Phillip E.
White.*

On March 31, 1997, Informix filed its annual financial report with the SEC. This report included SEC Form K-10, Informix's 1996 financial statement, and an independent auditor's report. As CEO of Informix, these forms were signed by White. This particular financial statement indicated that Informix had earned a net profit of approximately $98 million in 1996. This total amount included a contract with Fujitsu for $4.7 million, and with Hewlett-Packard (Europe) for $6.4 million.

The Fujitsu contract, which was signed in August of 1996, was for one year, and stipulated that all payments for products and services would be made within the time period of the contract. However, during his exit interview in late June 1997, the president of Informix-Japan produced a "side letter," wherein Fujitsu would be allowed to pay the total amount of money owed under the contract, in quarterly payments, through September 1998. This side-letter was issued reportedly without any authorization of White, Informix directors, or the Informix legal staff. Employees at Informix and/or their auditors determined that the 1996 financial statement was not correct, in that it listed income that Informix did not receive by the end of the year.

A few days later (on or about July 2, 1997), White became aware of a second side letter that existed in relation to the Hewlett-Packard contract, wherein Hewlett-Packard was granted the right to cancel the contract and be refunded any money they had paid to Informix. In fact, Hewlett-Packard wanted to cancel the contract and was demanding a return of monies that they had paid to date.

The discovery of the "side letters" impacted Informix's 1996 income, wherein the company would have to issue an amended 1996 earnings report. The issuance of an amended 1996 financial statement would drastically impact the value of the Informix stock, as well as possibly impact the future business and its standing in the high-tech industry, etc.

On July 4, 1997, White met with representatives of Fujitsu in Tokyo. As a result, a letter was written in which Fujitsu rescinded the side letter. Later that day, Informix entered into a Memorandum of Understanding (MOU) with Fujitsu. The MOU provided that Informix pay $3 million to Fujitsu for products and services (according to company documents, this amount approximately equaled the amount of money Informix was owed by Fujitsu).

On July 16, 1997, White as CEO of Informix, submitted a SEC Form S-8, in which he registered 12 million shares of Informix stock with the SEC for sale/distribution to Informix employees. In support of the Form S-8, the 1996 Informix financial statement was referenced.

On July 22, 1997, White resigned as Informix's President and CEO. On or about July 30, 1997, Informix's Board of Directors dismissed him from the board.

Auditors continued to re-examine Informix's transactions during 1996. The auditors determined that there were other "side letters" that had been issued regarding other contracts, as well as other accounting "irregularities" that would ultimately cause Informix to restate its 1996 income; they also concluded that Informix did not earn $98 million dollars in 1996, but instead lost $73 million.

Phillip White, as CEO of Informix, was responsible for submitting the SEC Form S-8 to the Securities and Exchange Commission in 1997. At the time the SEC Form S-8 was filed, Mr. White knew that the 1996 Informix earnings statement was inaccurate.[6]

The attorney's office acknowledged that Phil did not know of the side agreements and the fraudulent nature of these two deals until

June and July, well after the 1996 annual report had been submitted in March. Rather, it contended that Phil's actions after he became aware of the side letters were illegal.

The Fujitsu side letter executed by the president of Informix Japan secretly extended the payment terms of the $4.7 million deal by an additional year, thus making the revenue from this deal unrecognizable. Once Phil found out about the side letter, the prosecution argued, he executed his own side letter (MOU) with Fujitsu in order to have the first side letter rescinded. Then, he hid the MOU from the accounting department.

The side letter written by the Informix vice president in charge of Germany had granted HP the right to cancel the $6.4 million deal with Deutsche Telecom and receive a complete refund at any time. These additional terms made the revenue from this deal unrecognizable. Similarly, once Phil learned of the HP side letter, the prosecution claimed, he contacted senior executives at Hewlett-Packard in an attempt to also have it rescinded.

Knowing about these two side agreements and the fact that they adversely impacted Informix's financial position, Phil broke the law when he signed the SEC Form S-8. To further substantiate his unethical conduct, the government elaborated on the accounting irregularities that occurred under his leadership. The government claimed that a $98 million profit in 1996 was actually a $73 million loss.

It's hard to imagine that the CEO or board of directors at any billion-dollar company could know the exact details and legitimacy of every single dollar of revenue. The side letters that had been written for the $4.7 million Fujitsu deal and the $6.4 million HP deal had been executed by regional vice presidents. They were well hidden from senior sales management and the regional and corporate accounting departments. Even under today's stringent regulations of Sarbanes-Oxley (the finance legislation reform enacted in 2002 to enforce corporate fiscal accountability), these deals still would have passed inspection and been included as recognizable revenue. This is a disturbing thought indeed for anyone who serves as a board member or company officer.

The SEC requires more than two hundred different forms to be completed, depending upon a company's circumstances. The most familiar are the 10-K annual form, 10-Q quarterly report form, and S-1 initial offering stock registration form. In comparison to these forms, the S-8 form is of far less importance. It is considered a maintenance form and is routinely completed to add more shares of stock to a company's employee benefit plan. Regardless of their purpose and significance, all SEC forms are the same in that the filer's signature certifies its completeness and accuracy and reaffirms that the signer stands by the financial statements filed earlier. Whether inadvertently or on purpose, Phil broke the law when he signed the S-8 because he knew that Informix's previously filed financial statements were incorrect due to the side letters.

## THE DEFENSE ADDRESSES THE FUJITSU MOU

Phil White was represented by legendary lawyer John Keker and his fellow attorneys from the law firm of Keker and Van Nest. Best known for representing Oliver North in the Iran-Contra hearings, John Keker was mentioned most often when *California Lawyer* magazine surveyed attorneys about whom they would call if they were in trouble. "John Keker just may be the finest trial lawyer in the United States, and there are a lot of contenders for that," commented Michael Tigar, research professor at American University, Washington College of Law.[7] Phil had witnessed Keker's acumen firsthand when the lawyer represented Oracle against Informix in the lawsuit about the hiring of the Portland programmers.

The defense made the case that Phil was a leader "who was trying to do the right thing for his company under combat conditions. That he made a mistake is obvious. To blow it out of proportion is a product of politics, not law, common sense or clear thinking."[8] Phil's attorneys provided this account of events surrounding the MOU in their sentencing memorandum.

In June, 1997, with securities fraud suits brought by Milberg, Weiss and others already pending, Informix learned of a side-letter signed by a Japanese official, extending payment terms to Fujitsu for an extra year. Informix auditors, Ernst & Young, told White and others that the transaction, booked in 1996, would have to be debooked, triggering a restatement of 1996 financials, unless the side-letter was rescinded.

Informix's General Counsel, with the help of its Controller, drafted a rescission letter for Fujitsu, Informix's largest customer in Japan, to sign, and at Ernst & Young's suggestion White flew to Japan over the July 4 weekend to meet with Fujitsu.

In Japan, White met with Fujitsu representatives and told them he needed the rescission, and that the side-letter had not been known to or authorized by him or anyone else in the United States. During the discussion, both sides emphasized their on-going business relationships and need for mutual cooperation. Fujitsu was specifically interested in selling its products through Informix in the United States, and Informix was specifically interested (and had been for some time) in having Fujitsu replace Berlitz in the time-consuming and expensive process of translating Informix software products into Japanese computer speak.

The result was an agreement by Fujitsu to rescind the side-letter, which it did on July 4. The signed rescission was faxed to the United States on July 5, 1997. It was further agreed that Informix and Fujitsu representatives would continue to meet later that day to work out terms for Informix evaluating Fujitsu products and services. White left Japan and returned to the United States and did not participate in the later meeting. The result of the meeting was a memorandum of understanding (MOU) hammered out by top Informix managers in Japan, including the top financial representative.

That MOU is the basis of the allegation of the case. The accountants, when they learned of it, said it amounted to another side-letter (although they had told Informix and White in 1995 that MOU's could not be used as revenues, which makes it difficult to see how a nonbinding MOU could be another side-letter.)[9]

They argued that Phil had not concealed the MOU since Informix's general counsel (legal department head), David Stanley, was well aware of it. In addition, more than a dozen employees from the engineering department worked on the MOU details at the direction of their vice president. While Phil's attorneys tried to frame the MOU as the main premise for the government's case, they would still have to explain why Phil would knowingly sign an SEC document in light of the side agreements. They argued that it was an inadvertent mistake, since Informix's general counsel knew about the Fujitsu MOU, drafted the S-8 form, and told Phil to sign it.

## THE PROSECUTION TELLS A DIFFERENT STORY

The prosecution argued that Informix's auditors and finance staff had told Phil the signing of the S-8 would have to be postponed until the Fujitsu side agreement had been rescinded. When Phil volunteered to meet with Fujitsu, Informix's auditors, Ernst & Young, told Phil that the rescission letter had to be "clean" and that no consideration could be given to Fujitsu in order to achieve the rescission.

In court documents, the prosecution painted a picture of an unethical CEO who continually lied to company auditors and finance departments.

> White returned to the United States and provided the rescission letter to Informix's acting financial officer and Controller, as well as E&Y audit partner. White never disclosed the fact that he had to pay $3 million to Fujitsu in exchange for the rescission. Informix's acting financial officer telephoned White to ask how negotiations went. White stated that he obtained the rescission. When asked what the rescission cost, White responded: "Just a lot of aggravation."[10]

The attorney's office argued that Phil's concealment of the MOU was premeditated, took more than minimal planning, and should be punished accordingly. Phil was described as an unscrupulous leader: "His actions were deceptive, and violated every expectation of trust and integrity placed upon a Chief Executive Officer at a public company. The MOU was a direct betrayal of the company's finance officials in the United States, who had specifically told White that he could not give any concessions in negotiating a rescission of the 1996 Fujitsu side agreement."[11]

The prosecution also charged that Phil's behavior and misrepresentations in connection with the HP side agreement in the Deutsche Telecom deal constituted another illegal dealing. Although the prosecution acknowledged that Phil had not participated in the creation of the side letter, "White's efforts to negotiate away the HP side agreement are just as serious a breach of investor trust as the Fujitsu MOU."[12]

Upon learning of the HP side agreement, the prosecution argued, Phil met with various HP executives in an attempt to obtain a rescission and granted further verbal concessions to achieve his goal. However, the prosecution's timeline had some holes. For a day that the prosecution claimed Phil was meeting with a senior HP executive, Phil was able to prove he was at a doctor's appointment with his ailing mother. Ultimately, Judge Charles Breyer said, "The Hewlett-Packard incident plays no role and will not be considered as an important sentencing consideration."[13]

In addition to the HP Deutsche Telecom transaction, five more phony deals were uncovered by the audit that overstated revenue by $19.1 million. All of these deals originated from Informix's Germany offices. The SEC filed a civil complaint against Walter Königseder, the Informix vice president in charge of the region. The SEC charged that he had approved and ratified the secret side agreements. The commission served him in Germany, pursuant to the Hague Convention, and when Königseder failed to respond to the commission's complaint, the court entered a default judgment against him.[14] Efforts to extradite Königseder to the United States have been unsuccessful to date.

## THE GUILTY PLEA IN THE CRIMINAL CASE

Ultimately, Phil and his lawyers decided not to take the criminal case to trial and pled guilty. A trial where Phil's fate would be determined by a jury of average citizens was deemed too risky. The biggest risks were the composition of the jury and whether ordinary people would comprehend the complexities of financial accounting and the details of the case. Also, what would the jury members' personal reactions be toward Phil? Based upon the notoriety of the case and the negative press in the local papers, would they have already made up their minds that he was guilty?

In order to make an informed decision about a jury trial, the defense team decided to conduct a mock trial. In this type of hypothetical trial, the defense plays the role of both the prosecution and the defense to test how a sample jury would react to the respective arguments. The jurors are then observed as they deliberate, thus allowing the defense to learn their opinions and analysis of the issues.

The mock trial was a key factor in the defense team's decision not to take the case to trial. The results were mixed, and it seemed highly unlikely an impartial jury could be assembled that wouldn't be tainted in some way by the corporate scandals of the day: Enron, Worldcom, Adelphia, and Martha Stewart. An even greater concern was finding laypeople who could understand accounting and revenue recognition. Moreover, even if the defense could successfully convince a jury that the Fujitsu MOU was an innocent document, there was no getting around the fact that Phil had known about the two side letters when he signed the S-8. Based upon their past experiences with Judge Breyer, Phil's lawyers also believed that he would sentence Phil to the most lenient punishment. The decision was made—Phil would plead guilty.

Phil White pled guilty to count eight in the criminal case: aiding, abetting, and willfully causing false statements in a registration statement. Phil admitted his guilt in the following carefully worded statement:

> On July 16, 1997, I signed and Informix filed a SEC form S-8 with the SEC, registering 12 million shares of company stock for distribution to Informix employees. The S-8 incorporated Informix 1996 financial statements by reference. At the time I signed the S-8 and it was filed with the SEC, I knew that it was misleading with respect to material facts that the 1996 financial statements were in question and could have been restated to reflect a $6 million amount of revenue that could have been reversed related to the Fujitsu transaction.[15]

Following Phil's guilty plea, a United States probation officer was assigned to recommend an appropriate sentence to the court. The officer investigated Phil's past, visited his home, and interviewed him extensively. The statutory provisions for the offense allowed for a five-year jail term, up to three years of supervised release, up to five years of probation, and fines up to $250,000. However, the probation department recommended no jail time, no supervised release, one year of probation, a $10,000 fine, three hundred hours of community service, and a special assessment of $100. The United States probation officer wrote, "His conviction for this incident will prohibit him from serving on the board of a publicly traded company, and the media publicity generated by this event will also shade his future business ventures."[16]

## THE PROSECUTION SEEKS
## A PRISON SENTENCE

However, the attorney's office was under pressure to send white-collar criminals to jail. An article in the *San Francisco Chronicle* helps explain the office's situation and motivations: "The U.S. Attorney's office has done little to deter securities fraud in Silicon Valley, filing criminal charges against only a handful of high-tech executives the entire decade." The *San Francisco Chronicle* article further described the critical situation within the attorney's office: "Veteran prosecutors were leaving the office in droves. Case filings and conviction rates were plunging. And criminal referrals from the SEC and FBI were going unprosecuted."[17]

The assistant U.S. attorneys demanded that Phil's sentence include prison time. In their sentencing memorandum, they explained why the case merited imprisonment.

> The United States asks the Court to impose a three month sentence of imprisonment on the defendant Phillip E. White, the middle of the applicable guideline range. We do not make the recommendation lightly. This case is not about personal greed or dramatic market losses. White's offense conduct, however, reflects the kind of high-level corporate wrongdoing that has afflicted so many public companies, and which continues to undermine the investing public's faith in our securities markets.

White's decision to commit securities fraud savaged the reputation, and contributed to the downfall, of Informix, one of the country's most successful and promising high-technology companies. His decision to commit securities fraud also caused tangible harm to the company's customers and employees. He ignored the law, ignored his responsibilities as an officer, and purposefully deceived others whose job it was to protect investors and the integrity of Informix's financial reporting.

Simply stated, lying to the SEC and the investing public about financial results to falsely maintain the appearance of a company's success is a crime that requires strong punishment. A probationary sentence would not be sufficiently punitive and would severely undermine the principle of deterrence. Ultimately, the sentence in the case should not turn on whether White himself will re-offend. He probably will not. Instead, it should be imposed with an eye towards the hundreds of other officers of public companies in the Bay Area who are undoubtedly watching this case. They will ask themselves what the cost will be if they, like White, decide to report false financial results in the effort to stave off restatement or some other pending financial disaster for the company.[18]

The government's attorneys wanted to send a statement to the public that it was cracking down on the corporate accounting scandals that had become daily front-page news. In order to restore the faith of the investment community, they also wanted to prove that they were vigorously pursuing white-collar fraud. Finally, they wanted to use this case to create a deterrent and send a warning to other Silicon Valley CEOs, CFOs, and boards of directors who were undoubtedly following the ongoing developments. The warning was, if you break the law, you will go to jail.

The U.S. Attorney's Office also included a damning letter from Steven Cutler, director, SEC Division of Enforcement, in the sentencing memorandum: "Mr. White intentionally concealed this second side-agreement from Informix's internal auditors and independent accountants. Indeed, upon his return to California, Mr. White lied to Informix's internal accountants and independent auditors that he promised nothing in exchange for the Japanese customer's rescinding the first side agreement."[19] Cutler argued that Phil intentionally hid the Fujitsu MOU from Informix's accountants and lied about its contents. When the other side letters became public, a full sales audit was instituted. Per Cutler's letter, the restatements for year 1996 and previous years were a direct result of the audit findings.

Cutler also gave this accounting as to why the harsher penalties weren't enforced in the civil case:

> Mr. White recently made an offer of settlement to the Commission concerning the civil enforcement action against him, and the Commission's staff is recommending that settlement to the Commission. The settlement does not include civil money penalties because the limitations period has run on the Commission's claim. The allegations in the Commission's complaint, which Mr. White does not admit nor deny in his offer, go beyond the facts concerning the side agreement with the Japanese customer that Mr. White admitted to in his guilty plea. Nonetheless, the facts supporting his guilty plea constitute a serious violation of the federal securities law.[20]

He explained that the SEC settled because the time frame during which it could legally pursue the case was nearly expired.

Phil's attorneys wrote a vehement response to the assistant United States attorney regarding Cutler's letter: "We are troubled that several statements in Mr. Cutler's letter are just plain false."[21] They went on to refute Mr. Cutler's assertions:

While Mr. Cutler expresses concern regarding the concealment in connection with the Fujitsu Memorandum of
Understanding ("MOU"), the facts establish that the MOU
was negotiated by a senior member of Informix's financial
staff, Robert Dinsdale, Controller of Asia, and reviewed and
approved by Informix's General Counsel David Stanley.

Mr. Cutler's gratuitous discussion of the size of Informix
restatement is also grossly misleading, since virtually all of
the revenue restated by Informix was rebooked by the company in subsequent periods.

Mr. White did not lie about the MOU. To the contrary
he informed numerous Informix employees about it, including the general counsel, David Stanley, and Director of Product Development, Michael Saranga.

Mr. Cutler states that Mr. White "offered" to settle with
the SEC. I know personally that this statement is false. Mr.
White never made an offer to settle with the Securities and
Exchange Commission. To the contrary, after the Plea Agreement in the case had been negotiated, the SEC contacted us,
explaining that although the statute of limitations appeared
to have run out on a number of their claims, they were still
seeking an injunction against Mr. White.

The SEC then promptly proposed a Settlement Agreement in which Mr. White would admit nothing and would
be required to refrain from any future violation of securities
laws, an obligation that he would have anyway. There are no
financial penalties and no D&O bar.[22]

The two sides could not have had more divergent views of Phil's
actions and motives. Phil's attorneys made the case that Phil was
doing what any responsible leader would do after finding out about
the side letters when he tried to have the customers rescind them. He
was acting ethically and solely in the best interest of the company.

The assistant U.S. attorney presented an entirely different view: "Phillip White was not solely responsible for Informix's demise, but he played an indispensable role in its decline. 'Informix' is now synonymous with 'fraud' in Silicon Valley."[23] The attorney further argued that the case was "not about personal greed or dramatic market losses," but rather it was about a leader who was trying to create "the appearance of a company's success."[24] The U.S. probation officer made a similar observation and wrote about Phil's motivations in his sentencing recommendation report: "This officer can only surmise that Mr. White's involvement in this offense was based on his motivation to preserve his reputation in the high-tech community, as well as to maintain the appearance that Informix was a profitable and thriving entity."[25]

The defense team provided Judge Breyer with more than forty character reference letters, which they hoped would sway his opinion away from sending Phil to jail. They had letters from well-known leaders within the high-tech community and former Informix employees, including the former CFO and controller; the vice presidents of human resources, sales, marketing, and development; and many others. There were also letters from Phil's friends and his family.

After careful consideration, Judge Breyer sentenced Phillip E. White to two months in prison—a term one month shorter than the assistant U.S. attorney had requested and two months longer than the probation department's recommendation. While courts regularly accept the sentencing recommendations of the probation department, Judge Breyer rejected it in this case based upon principle.

*A judge must bear in mind that when he tries a case he is himself on trial.*

PHILO

# 8

# Lessons from Lompoc Prison

## AN INTERVIEW WITH PHIL WHITE

*Don't forget those who are in prison. Suffer with them as though you were there yourself.*

HEBREWS 13:3

Today, one out of every thirty-two Americans is either in jail or on supervised parole.[1] In August 2004, the United States federal prison roll call included 1,494 inmates housed at the correctional facilities in Lompoc.[2] One of these prisoners was Phillip E. White. The following interview with Phil took place at his home immediately before his incarceration. We spoke about his upbringing, his role at Informix, and the civil and criminal cases against him.

Phil's demeanor varied greatly during the several days of interviews. At times he was defiant, a man who truly believed he had done nothing wrong. At other times he seemed to be remorseful and in a state of disbelief that he was on his way to prison. He was very sorry about the pain and embarrassment he had caused Informix's employees, his friends, and most of all, his family. Although a stoic person by nature, he had moments of self-pity that he would be branded a felon for life. Conversely, he was upbeat and lighthearted when we talked about the early days of his career and the good times of Informix. True to form, he spoke honestly and didn't mince words on even the most sensitive subjects.

Q  *Pana, Illinois, is a long way from Silicon Valley. What kind of childhood did you have there?*

A  In a small town you really get to know people. You learn their traits and how to get a read on them. As a boy, I was an Eagle Scout and was always a very competitive athlete. I was also in all the speech and debating classes. I did a lot of plays and was a thespian. I believe that's why I could stand up in front of groups and present confidently. I think it made a big difference in my career.

My dad was an accountant but ran a pool hall where they held card games in the back room. For a school teacher to have a husband who ran a poolroom was quite something in a small town. My father died when I was in my early thirties. My brother was always closer to my dad because he liked all the gambling. I didn't like the crowd that was around it.

Q  *You are very particular about the type of people you hang around with?*

A  Yes, very particular. Usually older people—I seem to relate to them better. For example, when I ran tours in college I was always dealing with older people. They always trusted me and I felt more comfortable with them, more so than younger people. The older people had more experience and I could relate better to them. Throughout my career I would always befriend the older CEO or CIO.

Q  *How did your years at IBM impact your career?*

A  The first year and a half at IBM I was in training. Then I took over a territory in St. Louis and sold small machines. I still remember my first big sale and the letter I received from Tom Watson [IBM founder]. Because I always exceeded my sales goals, they kept giving me bigger and better territories. My goal was to always make my quota before I had met my FICA payroll deductions. I sold for six years and would always make my quota for the year by April.

More than anything, I wanted to be one of the top salespeople and make the Golden Circle Club. The salespeople who did 100 percent of quota went to Arizona or someplace like that. The Golden Circle Club winners went to some international location. You brought your wife along and they gave both of you all kinds of gifts. We did the same thing at Informix with Summit Club. Wives were always important to me. My philosophy has always been if the wife is happy, the guy is happy.

At IBM, if you didn't move about every eighteen months, your career was toast. After selling, I moved up to a regional staff position working on programs. I worked for Dave Hanna; his father ran Hanna-Barbera cartoons. I then advanced to branch manager in Oklahoma City and worked for George Conrades, who now heads Akamai.

My big career goal was to get to become a regional manager, and I continually interviewed with Mike Armstrong, who went on to run Hughes and AT&T. He was my business idol. I remember how he chewed me out once because I wore sweaters under my suit coat. That wasn't done at IBM, but I was always so damn cold! Finally, I was promoted to regional manager in St. Louis and then to a corporate marketing position in White Plains, New York. I decided to leave IBM instead of making the next logical career move, which would have meant moving to Japan. I joined Altos and moved to California instead.

*Q   What did you learn at Altos?*
A   The big thing I learned was how important VARs were. The other lesson I learned at Wyse was the importance of channels. We had retail, VARs, OEM, and direct. Software companies needed good hardware to run on. Altos provided the hardware and that's how I first met Roger Sippl. We convinced Sippl to port his database to our boxes.

I left Altos because Dave Jackson [Altos chairman] wouldn't make me president. I had been on the board of Wyse and they were doing a search for president. Bernie Tse [Wyse founder] was a good technician but needed some sales and marketing help. One of the board members suggested I do it.

Wyse built monitors and terminals and then decided to get into the PC business. I had this great idea of building the first computer that would never become obsolete. You would pull a bad board out and plug a new one in. We sold $50 million of them to Tandem in a big OEM deal. We also did a big deal with Businessland, the first big retail computer chain. We built them the first logoed boxes.

Q  *What I have read about your time at Wyse makes it sound like you missed the number, got sued, and ditched the company.*

A  We built the PCs in Taiwan and shipped them here to be reconfigured and burned in. That added extra months of time on everything. On top of that, the engineering was bad, and the boxes wouldn't work. We missed a quarter and got sued. We settled the lawsuit for around $15 million, I think, just to get rid of it. Bernie wanted to sell the company and move back to Taiwan. So we sold the company to a Taiwanese company called "Mytec," and I stayed on to help transition the company.

Sippl was looking for a president, but I hadn't really done much with him while I was with Wyse. They did a search and interviewed Bob Finocchio, myself, and a few others. Finocchio had worked at Informix as a consultant before he went to 3Com.

Q  *Why do you think you got the Informix job?*

A  I related better to the board members and had run a Silicon Valley company. There was a lot of rebuilding to do with the management team, and I think they thought I would hire better, and I was knowledgeable about sales and knew channels.

Sippl and I got along very well. I was good at sales and marketing, and he was good technically. I let him run all the technical stuff, and I became the spokesperson for the company. He's a very smart guy, but he didn't like to stand up in front of people and talk. Sippl's started a couple of other successful companies. He's also had to deal with some tough health problems and faced a lot of life's adversity. I liked him and have a lot of respect for him, but I also think he was too close to his people.

*Q   Did you keep a line between friends and business acquaintances?*
A   Yeah, I didn't want to make Sippl's mistake. I never socialized with anybody from work. I didn't do it at Altos, Wyse, or Informix. It causes less politics and doesn't make it seem like you are favoring someone. I never socialized individually. I didn't want people to think, "I'd better go out with White because something is going to happen if I don't." I would always go out as a group or have everyone together. For example, I would take the entire executive staff and wives out for a private Christmas celebration. I always bought their wives something nice. I made it a tradition for seven or eight years in a row, and the wives were always excited to come.

*Q   So, part of the strategy was to disassociate yourself personally from the people working with you?*
A   I think I learned that from watching others. I didn't want to fall into the trap of being too close to someone because I may have to fire them. That's why I don't do business with friends and I don't invest with friends. Because at some point in time, friendship ends. I think Sippl was friends with everybody.

*Q   What's the first thing you did at Informix?*
A   We had two of everything at Informix from the merger with Innovative: two headquarters, two R&D centers, two manufacturing

locations, two CFOs, and two heads of sales. I said we are going to shut down one of each and started moving the important functions to California.

Q  *But there were a couple of board members who were from Innovative Software.*

A  I had to change the board. I couldn't do anything while they were there, and that took time—about a year and a half. I started by making Menlo Park, not Lenexa, the headquarters. Then I named it the finance and development headquarters. Lenexa became the manufacturing and support site. It was quite a fight since the Innovative folks thought they were better at most everything. That's why they had to bring in a new president. Sippl had done well, but the board said, "The organization is really screwed up and we need somebody from the outside to sort it out."

Q  *Why did Sippl buy Innovative?*

A  I think he thought if he had desktop software, a spreadsheet, and office automation software, he could tie that back to the server. In a way, it was the start of client-server computing. However, he never got credit for it and the merger was a failure. But I think he had the right idea.

Q  *Did you think the idea of tying the desktop to the database was a good one at the time or did you think, "How in the hell am I going to turn this around?"*

A  I wanted to get rid of it day one. Informix had done well before Innovative, and we just needed to go back to the roots again. The merger cost the company a ton. Two years of everything—development, sales, and marketing. Wingz might have been the best graphical spreadsheet, but it was a commodity. To sell the product, you had to go to trade shows, give away bags, and do consumer advertising. We didn't do that at Informix.

*Q What did you think of the management team when you joined Informix?*

A Not much. I brought in a head of HR to help me hire. I brought in a new CFO and head of R&D. I brought in Mike Saranga, who had just retired from IBM. He built IBM's DB2, and I thought, he's going to be a real catch. He knew how to build databases for big iron. Saranga is really good, and he straightened out our R&D.

*Q What type of manager were you?*

A I basically let my team run their own show. However, I made them report weekly, quarterly, and put a lot pressure on them if it didn't look like they were going to make their promises. I'd force them to take action if they didn't move fast enough.

*Q It seemed like they wanted to please you, not just because you were the boss, but to earn your admiration.*

A You have to treat them well, respect them, and get to know their families. But you can't get too close to them. You get too close to them and they get to know you too well. You want to see if they can do what they say they can. If they can't, you are going to have to do something about it. If you try to help them do the job too much, you'll lose it all. Friends are outside business. Friends in business aren't friends forever. When things get tough, friendship dwindles.

*Q How was your relationship with the "new" board?*

A Once a year I would take the board members and their wives on a trip to another country. The board members liked it, and they got used to annually going away on an all-expenses-paid trip to Mexico, Tokyo, Singapore, or someplace. The board members never left, they always wanted to stay on board even during the toughest times. Nowadays, most people don't even want to be on a board because there is too much liability. You're signing documents that you have no way to tell are accurate.

*Q What do you think differentiated Informix from Oracle and Sybase?*

A  I built this company on relationships, and we were everybody's friend. I didn't know of anybody who didn't like Informix. I prided myself on good communications with the hardware, software, consulting, and application vendors. I think it really separated us from the rest of the pack.

*Q The press reported that there was $170 million of barter purchases in 1996, where Informix bought computer systems and in exchange the computer companies bought software.*

A  When we did our 1996 sales kickoff, I said we were going to spend $150 million to build superstores around the world so we could demonstrate applications on various platforms. If a customer wanted to see a particular system running SAP or PeopleSoft with Informix, we could demonstrate it to them. We were going to do it by vertical industry all around the world. We even put a big superstore center on Wall Street in the World Trade Center.

We began building out the superstores in '95. Initially, almost all the hardware vendors gave us the systems—HP, Sequent, Sun, NCR, Pyramid all gave us hardware. Then they said, we can't keep giving you these systems for free. So we started buying selected hardware systems, depending on the part of the world the superstore was in and what platform was popular there. In Mexico it was HP, and in Japan it was Fujitsu. When Oracle found out what we were doing, they started building them as well. They called it something else, but Ray Lane started it at the same time.

There was probably around $50 million of hardware purchased for superstores. The transactions were separate; that's why we could book them. While the hardware guys could ship me a box in a few days, it took us six to eight months to get their engineers and sales forces trained, put marketing programs in place, and tune our database for their boxes. The big challenge was getting the hardware providers' sales and support organizations to sell databases.

*Q   But weren't these quid pro quo purchases?*

A   I would say to them, "Hey, look, I'm going to buy your stuff and I expect you to do the same." They never were done concurrently. There's a lot of examples of other companies who have done the same. Sun buys $500,000 of Netscape and Netscape buys Sun servers. It happens all the time. That's why the auditors said it was okay, as long as there is a separate purchase order, you pay each other, and the discounts and time frames are different.

*Q   On the VAR side, Informix was doing pool-of-funds deals that some called "self-destructive."*

A   But if you had Baan software, Lawson, SAP, and all these companies selling software, every six months or nine months you would get another deal. It was good for everyone. It gave us a better relationship with all these software companies because they made money from our products. When they sold our licenses to end users, we could go in and sell other products behind it—data warehousing, tools, and services. It was a valid strategy. We were pretty successful at it because we didn't compete with them like Oracle and we understood partnerships unlike Sybase.

*Q   In hindsight, wouldn't it make sense when you did a $5 million pool of funds that the revenue be recognized over the term of the agreement?*

A   If we had changed the way we account for revenue, we would have had to stop and do exactly what Finocchio did. My big deal was that it locked Oracle out of the software and the hardware providers. We hurt them with this strategy. By the way, we only sold them OnLine 7.0. We had a lot more products to sell the customer. Our main problem was customer recognition and awareness. We just needed the customer to become familiar with Informix.

*Q   So then, why would Informix debook these pool-of-funds and superstore-related transactions?*
A   That's what's crazy. They were all paid for in advance. When they paid us, we recognized the revenue. The reason the auditors thought something was wrong was because the database licenses hadn't sold through. I kept telling them, "We are selling these engines in '96 but its going to be '97 or early '98 before they get sold through."

When the new management took over, they changed the way the revenue was recognized. They said, "When you ship it to the end user, that's how we are going to recognize the revenue. Everything that hasn't been shipped to an end user we're going to debook." However, they kept the money because it was already in the bank. It's kind of ironic that they wouldn't be collecting any money but would be counting the revenue.

The worst part about it is that they said it was all "bad business." I said, "How could this be bad revenue? You have collected the money, the customer is happy, and the strategy was not only to get them to sell our database but more importantly, to lock out Oracle." While I thought it was a great strategy they said, "It hasn't sold through so we are going to change the way we account and debook it."

*Q   The Informix-Illustra merger got great initial praise from the industry press. Do you think that it was because it wasn't Oracle?*
A   Well, it was going to be the most technically advanced database in the marketplace—way ahead of IBM, Microsoft, and Oracle. We spent four hundred million bucks buying what we thought was good technology. I trusted Stonebraker and Saranga and thought it would be ready for prime time in six months. At some point in time, things get pretty complicated and you have to trust the technical experts. We had the two best database minds in the business. I was thinking

we'll have the best database technology in the world, and we'll get a billion in revenue from it and kick some tail.

*Q   The sweet spot for Informix was UNIX. A lot of UNIX purists liked our products. One of the fundamental reasons they liked it was its adherence to ANSI SQL. Did you think people would migrate to Universal Server and its proprietary extensions when the world knows SQL?*

A   Well, I thought the ability to add all the content to the application would be compelling because all the application vendors were trying to make their software easier to use and understand. If you look at PeopleSoft, SAP, Baan, or Lawson, most of their installs were with us. So Illustra made sense, and we thought it was the next big wave.

*Q   But honestly, do you think any customers were excited about Illustra?*

A   Sure. They saw the beauty of Illustra.

*Q   At the time, it seemed like the internal focus of the company had shifted from OnLine Dynamic Server to Illustra overnight. Why did this happen?*

A   We bought them in December of '95 and it took about six months to get them integrated. The Illustra people wanted to spend too much money, do too much advertising, and hire too many people. I said, "Look, the product's not ready. You gotta stop it." It was disruptive, and their stuff wasn't working so I changed the Illustra management right after the sales kickoff in 1997. Then I got on Saranga and Stonebraker to figure out what was wrong.

*Q   Now there's a lot of buildup for Universal Server and it's not working.*

A   Yeah, I'm worried about it. Not many people knew the Illustra product wouldn't scale under any significant load. We kept it a secret. We had a good team of people working on it, and I was hopeful it would set the industry on its ear. I figured it might encourage Fujitsu,

IBM, or Microsoft to buy us. I honestly thought one of them would buy us in '98. We even talked about it several times at the board level and held talks with each of them. In fact, I believe that had we not missed our number in Q1 of '97, it would have happened. Because we'd give them 30 plus percent of UNIX market share, partnerships with all the application vendors, and we had a great development team.

Q *Oracle was still four times the size of Informix. Did you think Informix could defeat Oracle on its own?*
A I thought we were going to have to get bigger in the consulting business and potentially look at the application business. We needed more to sustain our level of growth. That's why I initially thought if we had the Illustra engine we may want to build our own applications or buy an application. There were a lot of companies that Informix could have bought to become like Oracle. Ultimately, I decided to stay away from applications because I didn't want to be like Oracle. We decided to focus on new engines and different complementary technologies.

Q *What else was on your mind at the end of 1996?*
A Howard Graham [Informix CFO] had left to become Siebel's CFO. They had just gone public at around $100 million in sales. He told me maybe a year or so before that he was leaving. I brought in a new CFO and he wasn't anything like Graham. Graham was more sales oriented. At the same time, we lost our audit team. Ernst & Young changed audit teams every seven years and they brought in another audit team. We lost our CFO, brought in another, and E&Y changed their audit team.

We had just come off a big year and ended about a billion in revenue. We're probably the fourth biggest software company in the world, behind Microsoft, Oracle, and SAP, and we had lots of changes going on. Plus the new technology wasn't ready, and we're sending the sales force out to sell it. In hindsight, we should have focused on Illustra as a lead-generation tool and kept selling the current engines.

Q   *Was there any inkling that Q1 of '97 would be a huge miss?*
A   Uh, no. I mean, my biggest worry was Illustra not being ready for prime time. I spent about a third of my time on Illustra. We had a lot of customers using it, and it wasn't scaling. It took bigger machines to run it on than we thought. We're spending a ton of money to promote it. Expenses were going up because we're hyping the hell out of it. We were putting too much engineering resource on it, from where I thought it should be at the time, and we're getting the sales force all cranked up to sell it. Two big mistakes.

You gotta sell what you got, and I thought the salespeople would use Illustra to open the door but sell the current engine. The problem is, they forgot to sell the products we had.

Q   *What was the catalyst for the internal sales audit? Was it missing*
    *the Q1 of '97 revenue number?*
A   The audit didn't come until April. Oh, yeah, and we missed it primarily in Europe. We had four or five major deals miss. There were a couple in Russia and a $30 million deal with Siemens. I was always optimistic and thought we were making it up through the end of March. Unfortunately, it all stopped.

Collections were slower than normal, and that's what caused all the problems in Europe. Everybody who owed us money for contracts was having a tough time selling it through. They used it as an opportunity to say, "We're not going to pay you." We put an audit team together and went over to Europe to find out if the contracts were good when they were written. We hired Baker & McKenzie, the largest law firm in the world, to audit the contracts to see what was wrong. Were the contracts bad? Were terms bad? Whatever? Basically, they came back and said that most of the contracts were valid; customers were just having a tough time selling it. It wasn't a whole bunch of bad contracts.

Q  *How could it be that you missed the quarter by such a huge amount?*
A  Several large enterprise deals didn't close. I had a big deal with EDS in the U.S. I was going to give them all of our internal operations, and they were going to resell our database everywhere in the world. It was a $30–$40 million deal. It didn't happen and ended up closing in the next quarter.

Q  *It's March 31 and you miss the quarter. What's the first thing on your mind?*
A  Call the Wilson Sonsoni law firm and say, "You gotta help me write a press release." We missed the number for the first time in twenty-eight quarters. Larry Sonsoni came over, and we called the board and told them the deals didn't happen, and we are going to put a press release out about missing the quarter. Usually, I called the board before the end of every quarter with good news. Their reaction was disbelief because I had always made it.

Q  *Usually a press release is done by the public relations firm. Why use a law firm to write it?*
A  Because the miss was big, and I knew we were going to get sued by Milberg Weiss. We put the press release out the day after the quarter ended. We came right back the next quarter and did $190 million. We came right back with big deals at Wal-Mart and others.

Q  *What was the reaction of the board?*
A  They're most worried about cash because I just paid $60 million for land to build the new corporate campus. We probably had a couple hundred million dollars cash in the bank. But if you think your revenue number is going to be up there, and your expenses are tied

to it, you burn a lot of cash in a hurry. We had layoffs and had to pay a lot of severances.

Q  *Then the board says, "Geez, Phil, what happened?"*
A  The company was a billion dollars, and we had always talked about bringing another guy in because I had all the titles. So we started looking for potential candidates for president. I knew Ed Zander, the COO of Sun, and Dave Dorman, who ran Pacific Bell.

Q  *Was that the board's suggestion or your suggestion?*
A  I wanted to bring somebody else in as president, although I wasn't ready to give up the CEO spot yet.

Q  *If you had made the Q1 number, would you still have done that?*
A  Yeah, the company was getting too big. I mean, I couldn't take all the travel, manage all the technology, and the staff was getting big. We were acquiring companies. There was too much to do. You can't run the world at a billion and a half dollars. Traveling around the world was just too much. I had traveled four million miles on airlines, causing one divorce, and I didn't want it to cause another one. It was time.

We had to find the right person, and I put the names in a hat. We would divide the company up. One of us would take finance, R&D, and the other, sales and marketing. I would have taken sales and marketing. The three guys we ultimately brought into the fold were Dorman, Zander, and Bob Finocchio. But it was hard to attract someone who wanted to be president with me still there as CEO. So I said, "I'll be chairman."

Q  *You obviously thought Finocchio would do a good job if you brought him in.*
A  Well, I didn't know much about him. He was the number two guy at 3Com. So I called Finocchio and asked him if he would like

to talk to me about working at Informix. I also called Dorman because that was the same time SBC was buying Pacific Bell.

Q  *Did these guys think, "Why would I come to Informix. You just missed the last quarter"?*
A  No. The stock was way down. It was a great opportunity to make a lot of money.

Dorman wanted it the most, I thought, because Finocchio wasn't working and he had made a lot of money at 3Com. Dorman liked the software industry, and I thought he could make a big difference for us in telecom.

Q  *Who did you want to become president?*
A  I wanted Dorman, and it came down to Finocchio and him. The board's choice was Finocchio. They rationalized that he had been in a smaller business and knew more about technology. Dorman was from a bigger company and wasn't from the software industry.

Q  *Do you think this decision was made by the board to become independent from Phil White?*
A  No, I think they truly believed that Dorman was too much above running a small company. We had 4,000 people and he had 80,000.

Q  *So the board, not Phil White, chose Finocchio.*
A  Yes.

Q  *Was this the first time in all the years that you "lost" a decision to the board?*
A  First time. They would have let me buy a jet if I had wanted. We had a $30 million venture fund and bought a new building. But I think they thought the company was slowing down. We're getting sued and the lawsuits are big. I am sure they thought, "We need to

have a new CEO to minimize the damage from the lawsuits." The board thought we needed to make a perceived difference to the outside world. I agreed with that.

I argued that Dorman would be perfect for the job. He knew everyone in telco, and we would own that market. He wanted the job, and we met a lot to talk about it. We had been friends, and I played golf with him. It was the first and last time the board ever disagreed with my decision. Finocchio knew I didn't want him.

*Q  What was it like between the time when Finocchio came on board and you resigned?*

A  It was the end of June when he came on board, and I announced him at the user conference in the middle of July. Many people think I resigned. I hired him to be the president and CEO. I was still chairman.

*Q  Did you like him?*

A  No.

*Q  Did he like you?*

A  I don't think so. Finocchio and I didn't get along—not at all.

*Q  During this whole time frame, while the Fujitsu MOU is going on, how big an item is this on your radar?*

A  It wasn't, because I didn't know anything about it till the end of June. Bill James [new head of Informix Japan] was doing an exit interview with Norio Murakami [previous head of Japan] and he told him that he signed a side letter with a schoolmate at Fujitsu. The auditors told us we were going to have to debook the Fujitsu deal for the fourth quarter of '96 and restate the quarter. So I asked the auditors if there was anything we could do. They said, "Get Fujitsu to sign a rescission that says they'll pay it."

*Q   With the Q1 sales disaster, you didn't want to restate Q4?*

A   Yes, that would have meant more lawsuits. I didn't want to go to Japan since there was too much going on at corporate. But James was brand new and didn't know the Fujitsu people. Stanley [Informix legal counsel] was up with the Oracle lawsuits when they hired Gary Kelly. There wasn't anybody else left to go so I had to go. The Fujitsu deal was about four and a half million, and they had burned off about 20 percent. So they owed about three and a half million.

*Q   So the deal coming back on the MOU was . . . ?*

A   Rescind the side letter, which they did. The MOU basically said we would look at buying some of the products and services, primarily localizing our products. At the time we were paying Berlitz four to five hundred thousand dollars a product to localize. We had about eight products, on both UNIX and NT, Fujitsu could localize and improve for us. So they signed the MOU and faxed it to my house. I took it to the office and gave it to Stanley. Saranga's organization started to work on the details, and a localization team was sent to Japan.

Ultimately, Fujitsu burned it all off and paid for all of it. Furthermore, Finocchio hired them to complete the localization that was in the MOU in the first place. My thinking was if Fujitsu localizes our products, they might be more inclined to buy the company because the products would look like theirs. They wanted a software company.

*Q   Did it occur to you to give it to accounting? Wouldn't you have given it to Howard Graham if he had still been there?*

A   Probably not. I gave it to Stanley and Saranga. Once you give it to the legal counsel, they know about the MOU and they knew about Fujitsu. If they would have thought there was something wrong with it, they would have taken it to the auditors and accountants. We had about fifteen other people in the company looking at Fujitsu products and services so that we could decide something by September. There weren't any commitments on our side, and we had sixty days to decide to move forward with the MOU.

*Q   Did Fujitsu think the MOU was in fact a side letter?*
A   They probably thought it was more serious than I did. I thought we had done a great job and saved the deal.

*Q   Getting them to rescind the side letter was the goal?*
A   They rescinded it. The auditors had specifically told us a year before that you couldn't book anything on an MOU, so I didn't see anything wrong and got on with business. We scheduled a meeting on the last day of the user conference at the end of July for Fujitsu to come over and meet with Saranga to see if there was any technology we wanted of theirs and to talk about the localization.

*Q   Then what happened?*
A   The office manager in Japan was sending over all the stuff at the end of the month and sent the MOU over. He had already communicated with Stanley about putting it on letterhead. The finance people saw it and said it was a side letter. About two hours before the board meeting that had been previously scheduled for that night, I met with Finocchio and Stanley and argued that it wasn't a side letter. It was an MOU and Stanley's had it for a month. What ultimately happened was Finocchio took it to the board that evening and said it was a side letter and the reason we got the rescission letter from Fujitsu. He said, "Either White goes or I go."

The MOU was done on July 4 and on the 16th Stanley had given me an S-8 to sign in order to update our employee stock purchase plan. I don't even remember signing the S-8. I assume that was because it was about a week before six thousand customers would be attending our user conference. Stanley signed it, gave it to me, and I signed it. I always signed everything he signed. He knew about the MOU and he knew about the rescission letter, so I didn't give it a second thought. In fact, he put the MOU on letterhead because it had been written in Japan on plain paper. He typed it, I signed it, and sent it to Japan.

*Q OK, so that's where some of the charges come from?*
A Wire fraud and mail fraud. Wire fraud because they faxed it to me and mail fraud because we mailed it back. Isn't that unbelievable?

*Q Did anyone warn you not to sign the S-8?*
A The S-8 was signed two weeks after the MOU was signed. I received it from our general counsel, who had prepared and signed it. He was responsible for the document and all correspondence with the SEC. The accounting and finance departments never even looked at the S-8. So, if there was a concern about the MOU or the S-8, you would think he wouldn't have signed the S-8 and sent it to me for my signature.

*Q So, the charges weren't related to signing any quarterly statements?*
A No. When you sign an S-8, which I didn't know at the time, you validate by representation of your signature that the numbers haven't changed. The SEC actually dropped their case. The statute of limitations was running out and they did tolling agreements, which extended the statute of limitations by short periods of time. They stopped doing tolling agreements, which extended their time frame to prosecute and proposed a settlement. In the meantime, there were four U.S. district attorneys over eight years who didn't do anything with my case. Then a new district attorney came in, and you had Enron, WorldCom, and everything else happened. He had to pursue my case.

Q *But if they dropped the case, why did you sign an SEC settlement document?*

A The settlement was what they gave me that says they're done. I signed it because all it said was that I wouldn't violate any securities laws. There wasn't any fine, no director-and-officer disbarment. That's what usually happens. They didn't do anything.

So when John Keker [Phil's attorney] and I decided what we were going to do in the criminal case, instead of going to trial, we thought it might be better to plead to signing the S-8. He said, "You won't do any time because I know Judge Breyer and there's not enough points." I pleaded guilty to signing an S-8 that "potentially"—that's exactly what I said, "potentially"—could have been construed by the auditors as a side letter and potentially force me to restate. I didn't say "would" because the SEC had dropped the case.

Should I have gone to trial? It's pretty dicey to talk about complex accounting issues with people off the street. I thought that after the SEC dropped their case, the judge would give me a little fine, maybe $10,000, and a hundred hours of community service, which was the probation department's recommendation. Usually judges follow its recommendations. For example, in the case of Martha Stewart, the judge said the probation officer's report made him give her the minimum he could give her—ten months, five in prison, five out.

Q *Now you've pleaded guilty to signing an S-8, and you're in deep trouble.*

A I can't talk publicly and tell everyone what happened. The U.S. attorney never deposed me or even talked to me. It was all done through lawyers. I think their motivation was to go after white-collar crime and make a name in the Valley. Also, my lawyer was the "Enron guy." Keker represented Fastow, the Enron CFO, and Frank Quattrone, the infamous Credit Suisse First Boston investment banker.

*Q   What did you think of Keker?*
A   He's the lawyer that lawyers go to when they are in trouble. He was a marine who was shot in Vietnam. Doesn't take any crap from anybody. He swears a lot and it's very effective too.

*Q   So you pled guilty?*
A   My plea says I did not tell the auditors that I signed an MOU when I signed an S-8. One of the key points I told the judge at sentencing was that the company ultimately sold for a billion dollars to IBM. Think of another company with financial problems that sold for a billion dollars. The employees liked it because they received better benefits and were now part of a bigger, more stable company. There was no loss to the shareholders, and the government agreed to that. I made very little money personally and left the company with three times the stock that I started with. And there were no actions by the SEC. I asked the judge to take all these into consideration and go by the probation department's report. He said that he understood.

*Q   But it seems there was a miscalculation on Keker's part on
    the sentence.*
A   Yeah, he couldn't believe it. He said, "I have known this judge for thirty years. He'll go by the probation report. It will be a short meeting, in and out." We go in and the judge says, "I am considering giving you jail time. But I'll give you an opportunity to come and talk about it." I came back two weeks later and gave him a presentation.

He said he thought long and hard about this but that he needed to make an example out of me. Then he went into a dissertation about how he put many people in jail. His point was that he has put a lot of people in jail for a lot of different things. Sixty days in jail isn't bad because this place has "a workout facility and a salad bar"— his exact words.

*Q  On the surface, it seems like he had to give you jail time.*
*If he hadn't, the newspapers would have been all over it.*

A  Yes, the newspaper headlines were all about the ex-CEO who goes
to jail. The newspapers didn't say, "White goes to jail for sixty days."
They said, "White goes to prison!" I think he was very politically
motivated to get something for the Justice Department so they could
say they put a guy in jail and make themselves look good. His brother
is on the Supreme Court, so you would think he has ambitions to
move up to a higher court. He had to look like he's tough on white-
collar crime.

*Q  Finocchio wrote a letter very critical of your actions to the judge*
*at the time of your sentencing.*

A  The character reference letters from former key Informix executives were all positive and supportive. I believe when the prosecutor
saw them, he asked the SEC director and Finocchio to write letters.
Why didn't he get over it? I don't know.

*Q  The SEC director also wrote a letter to the judge at the sentencing*
*that talked about the MOU and side letters in Europe.*

A  I honestly don't think the SEC director wrote that letter. I am
convinced that the letter was ghostwritten. His assistant even signed
it for him. I am convinced that when Robbins [assistant U.S. attor-
ney] saw the good letters, especially the ones from the Informix
accounting team, he thought the judge would let me off. Keker shares
that opinion, and he wrote about it in his response.

I didn't know about the side agreements in Germany. Four or five
days before I left Informix, I sat down with Königseder and asked
him if there were any more side letters than the one we had found
out about. He said, "Absolutely not," and that wasn't the truth. There
were five or six. The day I left the company was the day I found out
about the side letter he did with HP.

*Q   Why do you think sales guys like Walter Königseder write side letters?*

A   Pressure. You gotta make the number and you don't want to disappoint. If a manager does it, then it descends down to the salespeople. It went down from Königseder to the manager running the east bloc, the managers running Germany and Russia.

Side letters are also a cultural issue. In countries like Japan and Germany, these people have known each other for life. Königseder knew every guy he did a side letter with. In Japan, Murakami did his side letter with a schoolmate. SAP and Sybase also had terrible problems with side letters in Japan.

*Q   On one hand, it makes sense for Finocchio to restate revenues, but in many cases a restatement of that size is the death sentence for a software company. Also, from a personal perspective, his stock options would be way above water. Why'd he do it, then?*

A   Customers weren't paying so they started looking at what wasn't sold through. This made his job easy. Just go back and debook everything that hadn't been sold through. Make it a big number and be done with it. Then, as it sold through, rebook it.

If he could continue to sell new licenses and rebook the stuff that had been sold over the last three years, while there wouldn't be any cash, revenue would be up and he would look like a hero. However, he couldn't keep the new license sales up.

*Q   Was there any reason in your mind for Informix to debook the $311 million in business?*

A   No. It had been paid for. There are two reasons they did it. One, they didn't want to keep the auditors looking for other bad transactions and this was a way to sweep it up all at once. Two, it allowed them to have a great windfall. Ironically, they would have to restate a few months later.

Q  *But Finocchio probably doesn't consider it a change of accounting. It was his fiduciary duty to clean up the books.*

A  I did it in '91; he did it in '97. Ninety percent of all the "bad business" he debooked he got to rebook. Had I called the lawyers who won $142 million in the class-action suit and told them about this, they would have sued them again for rebooking the stuff they said was bad business.

Q  *In hindsight, is there anything you could have done to prevent this entire episode from happening?*

A  Several things. I could have given the MOU to the accounting team. At the board meeting on the night of the twenty-eighth, I could have stood up and talked about the MOU and explained what exactly happened. I think that would have stopped it. The real issue is that we should have had Dorman in the office, not Finocchio. I should have gone with my gut and pushed harder for him.

In hindsight, time doesn't help. Look what happened to me. In 1997 there wasn't Enron, Worldcom, Adelphia, and all the other white-collar stuff. Time hurt me. Later, they wanted to prove something and got me on the smallest technicality. If you talk to any CFO, they'll tell you that nobody looks at an S-8. The auditors don't ever look at an S-8 and I don't even remember signing the damn thing!

Q  *How about the Illustra acquisition in hindsight? Buy or no buy?*

A  No buy. But it was hard when you had Saranga and Stonebraker, the brightest two minds in the database business, saying it's a good deal. Saranga was really pushing me to do it after he tried to do it himself. It could have pushed over time to be the bigger, better database company than Oracle. It would have allowed us to sell the company for a lot of money. In '97 we were a billion in revenue and our market cap was three or four billion then. We would have fetched a bundle.

Q  *But was the Illustra acquisition your "brainchild," for a lack of*
   *better words?*
A  Yeah, and guess who helped me buy it—Frank Quattrone [for-
mer head of Credit Suisse First Boston's technology banking business
who was sentenced to eighteen months in prison for obstructing justice and witness tampering in 2004]. Another one of Keker's clients.

Q  *Did you honestly believe you could defeat Oracle?*
A  Yes.

Q  *Biggest mistake?*
A  The big mistake is that I misjudged the technical readiness of the
Illustra product. OnLine was doing great, and we had all the appli-
cation guys in our court.

   Ultimately, I still believe I didn't do anything wrong. To be put in
jail over an MOU that I had nothing to do with in the first place is
pretty harsh, I think. All I was trying to do was protect the company.

Q  *Informix was called the "last true database company." Was there*
   *a future for the last true database company?*
A  Yeah, because if you remember we weren't running that well on
NT yet. NT was migrating to bigger systems on multiprocessor boxes.
That was another whole market, and then Linux was coming, even
though it wasn't a big deal at the time. The Internet boom was starting and Illustra was the Internet engine.

   We could have kept running the company or sold it for a lot of
money. I had offers to do lots of other stuff—run hardware companies and other big software companies—but I didn't want to leave. I
had people asking me to sit on big boards because every major company wanted a technology guy on the board. But I lost all that once
I got indicted. They didn't want to have to put that in their 10-K.
Even though I can be a director and an officer today, you would still
have to make it public that I am a felon. Anybody who doesn't know

me personally would say no way. While I can legally still run a company, I really can't. I can't even vote, and I probably couldn't get a loan if I ever had to.

*Q  Is your sentence a deterrent to other CEOs in a similar situation?*
A   If you're running a company and you hear I get a $10,000 fine and sixty days in jail, is that going to influence what you do? Get a $20 million fine and that will attract attention.

*Q  Why did you agree to participate in this book?*
A   Well, I thought all along about doing a book, primarily for my kids. When they are older, I thought they would want to learn about it. I was going to write it myself because I think it had to include the entire experience. Because you were with Informix during this entire time, it was only natural to participate in your book.

I also feel I have a story to tell about the perils of running a public company. I think others who are caught in a similar situation would want to talk to me about lawyers, boards, the SEC, and the criminal side. Not many people know much about points, judges, and court.

*Q  Was Informix the best job you ever had?*
A   Yes.

## PHIL WHITE'S LESSONS LEARNED

I met with Phil White once again just after his release from prison. He was in good spirits and relieved to have his "debt to society" paid in full and behind him. He was also noticeably thinner, having lost twenty pounds. He told me that he thought his time in prison was much harder on his family than it actually was for him. He philosophized that it was the first time he had been truly alone to reflect upon his life and think about the future.

I asked Phil to explain the business and leadership lessons he has learned from his entire ordeal. Here's what he said.

- Fame to blame. The press builds you up and tears you down. The blame is always bigger than what it really is. Your relationship with your kids, family, business colleagues, and friends changes. Because of the legal proceedings, you don't have the opportunity to explain your side of the story and what really happened.

- Small keep all. When you're a small company with sales to a half billion, keep all the titles—president, CEO, and chairman. When you get bigger, bring in a COO, somebody you can test, and start some progression of offloading some of the business areas.

- Say no to the yes-man. Your CFO has to be his own guy, someone who will stand up to you. The other senior staff usually won't. The CEO and CFO have got to get along, and I learned this the hard way.

- When troubles begin, friendships may end. People who you thought were your friends aren't. No one will stand up for you because everybody wants to cover their own hide. Today, a lot of the big-name guys who I thought were friends don't want to be associated with me. Other people believe only what they have read. Only the people who worked with me really know me.

- Time does not cure all ills. The lesson is to get bad stuff over with quickly. In 1997, this would have blown over. In 2004, everyone wanted to get Ebbers, Lay, Fastow, and White for their own reasons.

- The buck stops with the CEO. Even though Informix's legal counsel knew about the Fujitsu MOU, participated in its creation, and signed the S-8, I was held solely accountable. As CEO, you must pay attention to all the details because you will be held accountable for all the details.[3]

*You never really understand a person until you consider things from his point of view . . . 'til you climb inside of his skin and walk around in it.*

ATTICUS FINCH, IN HARPER LEE'S *To Kill a Mockingbird*

# Epilogue

## THE REAL STORY

JUDGE BREYER MADE the following comments at the time of Phil's sentencing:

> I will tell you what my present view of your client is. I think he is a good person. I think he has done a number of things in his life that are laudable, exemplary. I think he is a good family man. I think he has a number of friends. I think he has a sense of conscience. I think he has a sense of community. I think he has all those things. Also, I think there is no likelihood at all that he would repeat this conduct.
>
> Having said that, I think he did a very bad thing and I think that a sentence in some measure has to send a signal, not to him because he has heard the signal. I think it has to send a signal to the community out there which, in my view is the following: if a person in that position of responsibility knowingly signs or has reason to believe, in this case he certainly did, that the statement is false, and submits it to the government, then that is worthy of jail. That is the message I want to send. I want to make sure that people who file these forms understand that if it is false, then it is worthy of jail.[1]

Judge Breyer's character assessment of Phil White is quite correct. He certainly isn't your typical ex-convict. Undoubtedly, most business leaders could also be described using Judge Breyer's terms—they are good people with consciences who care for their families. However, the difference between greatness and infamy has never been smaller for today's business leaders. Under the business climate of Sarbanes-Oxley, officers risk losing not only their careers but also their freedom, every time they sign off on their company's numbers. This is one of the reasons that make the real story of Informix so disturbing.

Back in 1991, no one could have imagined the spectacular rise and fall of Informix or the fact that Phil White would wind up in prison. Phil ended up in jail through a series of circumstances of his own creation. These circumstances could happen to any CEO who pays more attention to personal accolades than to the details of running a business. And unfortunately, history has a way of repeating itself.

The media that once proclaimed Phil White a hero now regard him as the poster boy for Silicon Valley greed. However, the media missed the story. The real story is about the Silicon Valley value system, where the pecking order is based upon press clippings and net worth is far more important than self-worth.

In fact, the media are a key part of the story. They continually determine who's hot and who's not. They were equally motivated to promote the hero worship of Phil White as his star was rising and then to lead the campaign to vilify him when times turned bad. In the process, they edited and generalized any facts that would have detracted from either of these crusades.

In the end, the chroniclers of history's controversial events determine how these events are remembered. Until this time, only the press has written the story of Informix. To those of us who were there, the press got it wrong. We agree with David Shaw of the *Los Angeles Times* when he wrote, "The public thinks the press is too negative, too cynical, too interested in sensationalizing and trivializing the news. They think the press is biased. They think that whenever the press covers a story that they, the readers and viewers, know something about personally, the press gets it wrong."[2]

Unfortunately, the press did get the Informix story wrong. Informix was a great company filled with ethical employees who overcame incredible adversity to grow the company to nearly a billion dollars in sales. The companywide fraud on the immense scale that the press reported about simply didn't happen. People with Informix on their résumés should be respected for the company's achievements, not looked upon with skepticism or distrust. My hope is history will regard this book as the final word on Informix.

However, the final chapter on Phil White has yet to be written. The history books are full of exiled heroes who faded into oblivion. Bouncing back from disaster takes courage, confidence, and humility. A true hero takes life's worst experiences and uses them to help others. In this regard, only Phil White can write the final chapter of his story.

*Let him be the best of men, and let him be thought the worst; then he will have been put to the proof; and we shall see whether he will be affected by the fear of infamy and its consequences.*

PLATO

# Notes

## Introduction

1. Sean Silverthorne, "Can Informix Get the Red Out?" *Times Tribune,* May 22, 1989.
2. Reynolds Holding and William Carlsen, "Hollow Words," *San Francisco Chronicle,* November 16, 1999.
3. Lori Pizzani, "The Anatomy of an Earnings Restatement," *The Financial Journalist,* June 2003, http://www.cfainstitute.org/pressroom/fjnews/fjjjao3.html (accessed July 3, 2004).
4. United States Securities and Exchange Commission, "Litigation Releases," United States Securities and Exchange Commission Database, http://www.sec.gov/litigation/litreleases.shtml (accessed June 20, 2004).
5. Marc L. Songini, "I2 Wraps Up Reaudit, Restates Earnings for Four Years," *Computerworld,* July 22, 2003, http://www.computerworld.com/softwaretopics/erp/story/0,10801,83315,00.html (accessed July 1, 2004).
6. John Coffee Jr., "Gatekeeper Failure and Reform: The Challenge of Fashioning Relevant Reforms," University of California, March 1, 2004, http://repositories.cdlib.org/blewp/art160/ (accessed July 8, 2004).
7. Stanford Law School, "Informix Corporation—Company and Case Information," Stanford University, http://securities.stanford.edu/1008/IFMX/ (accessed July 2, 2004).
8. Holding and Carlsen, "Hollow Words."
9. United States Securities and Exchange Commission, "Litigation Releases."

10. Customer Management Zone, "Ghost of Informix Rises in Accounting Scandal Indictment as CEO Faces Jail Threat," Insightexec.com, November 25, 2002, http://crm.insightexec.com/cgi-bin/item.cgi?id=97414 (accessed June 28, 2004).

11. Stanford Law School, "United States District Court Class-action Lawsuit No. C-98-0437-FMS," Stanford University, http://securities.stanford.edu/1008/IFMX/23003.htm (accessed June 25, 2004).

12. U.S. Attorney's Office, Northern District of California, press release, May 26, 2004, http://www.usdoj.gov/usao/can/press/html/2004_05white.html.

13. Joe Lumbley, "Informix 'Fire Sale' Has Investors Irked," *Database Dev Zone,* April 27, 2001, http://archive.devx.com/free/newsletters/dbzone/dbednote/dbednote042501.asp (accessed July 6, 2004).

# Chapter 1

1. Mary Eisenhart, "Informix at 10: Meeting the Corporate Database Challenge," *Microtimes,* February 5, 1990.

2. Ibid.

3. Ibid.

4. Ibid.

5. United States Census Bureau, "2000 Censtats Database," http://censtats.census.gov/data/IL/1601757472.pdf (accessed June 4, 2004).

6. Kathleen Doler, "Informix's Phil White: Converting Personal Ambition into Companywide Success," *Investors Business Daily,* November 29, 1994.

7. Julie Pitta, "Altos Senior VP Resigns to Become Wyse's President," *Computer System News,* May 12, 1986.

8. Ibid.

9. Ibid.

10. Class Action Reporter, "Headlines," Vol. 1, No. 210, November 30, 1999, http://www.bankrupt.com/CAR_Public/991130.MBX, Inter Net Bankruptcy Library (accessed May 1, 2004).

11. Eisenhart, "Informix at 10."

12. Andrew Auld, "Informix Forges a Comeback," *UnixWorld,* November 1989.

13. Informix Software, Inc., 1989 Informix Annual Report (1989).
14. Auld, "Informix Forges a Comeback."
15. Joshua Greenbaum, "The CA-Way Works," *Software Magazine,* February 1998.
16. Silverthorne, "Can Informix Get The Red Out?"
17. Auld, "Informix Forges a Comeback."
18. Silverthorne, "Can Informix Get the Red Out?"
19. Tony Kyne, "Help!" Google, October 4, 1991, http://groups-beta
    .google.com/group/comp.os.vms/browse_frm/thread/8b46e3a6888410
    69/94c05fc1977dad03?q=Tony+Kyne+sworn&rnum=1#94c05fc1977d
    ad03 (accessed June 3, 2004).
20. Auld, "Informix Forges a Comeback."
21. Informix Software, Inc., 1990 Informix Annual Report (1990).
22. Yanik Crepeau, "If DBkit Is So Great," Google, June 10, 1993,
    http://groups.google.com/groups?q=oracle+revenue+1990&start=10
    &hl=en&lr=&ie=UTF-8&selm=1993Jun10.221418.2267%40CAM
    .ORG!planon&rnum=14 (accessed May13, 2004).
23. "UnixWorld's Top 10," *UnixWorld,* December 1992.
24. Jeff Mann, "Ingres for A/UX," Google, January 28, 1992, http://groups
    .google.com/groups?q=informix+1991&start=20&hl=en&lr=&ie=UTF
    -8&selm=1992Jan28.171501.12828%40intacc.uucp&rnum=26
    (accessed May 21, 2004).
25. "Newsletter," November 1991, Washburn University, http://www
    .washburn.edu/its/newsletters/news (accessed May 13, 2004).
26. Informix Software, Inc., 1991 Informix Annual Report (1991).
27. Kathleen Pender, "Informix Corp. Stock Surged 448%," *San Francisco Chronicle,* April 20, 1992.
28. "Newsletter," November 1991.

## Chapter 2

1. Frank Hayes, "Who Says the Hostilities Are Over?" *UnixWorld,* December 1992.
2. Jim Ericson, "IBM Edges Oracle in DMBS Market," *Line56,* May 8, 2002, http://www.line56.com/articles/?ArticleID=3656 (accessed June 3, 2004).

3. William R. Boulton, "Compaq Computer Corporation: Initiating a Price War," Auburn University, 1993, http://www.business.auburn.edu/~boultwr/compaq1.pdf#search='boulton%20compaq%20price%20wa' (accessed May 21, 2004).

4. Department of Mathematics and Computer Science, "UNIX Chronology," University of Udine, http://www.dimi.uniud.it/~miculan/Didattica/UNIX-history.html (accessed May 23, 2004).

5. Steve Kaufman, "Attention to Detail Spurs Stunning Turnaround," *San Jose Mercury News,* August 24, 1992.

6. Eric Nee, "Informix Is Back," *Upside Magazine,* June 1993.

7. Florencia Lafuente, "Popcorn, Popcorn, Popcorn," *Apertura Magazine,* January 1995.

8. Informix Software, Inc., 1990 Informix Annual Report (1990).

9. Miranda Ewell, "Informix Settles Fraud Suit," *San Jose Mercury News,* May 27, 1999.

10. Alorie Gilbert, "Oracle Cuts Rewards for Last-minute Deals," *CNET News,* June 19, 2002, http://news.com.com/2100-1017-937593.html?part= msnbc-cnet (accessed June 4, 2004).

11. Martin Garvey, "Vendors Held Accountable," *InformationWeek,* April 29, 1991.

12. Ibid.

13. Nee, "Informix Is Back."

14. Malcom Gladwell, *The Tipping Point* (Boston: Little, Brown and Company, 2000).

15. Martin Rosenberg, "Informix to Give Bonus to Reward Employees," *Kansas City Star,* November 4, 1992.

16. Ibid.

17. Informix Software, "Informix Software Elects New Chairman of Board of Directors," news release, December 16, 1992.

18. Kaufman, "Attention to Detail Spurs Stunning Turnaround."

19. Ibid.

## Chapter 3

1. Nee, "Informix Is Back."

2. "Silicon Valley 150," *San Jose Mercury News,* April 12, 1993.

3. "The Times Top 100," *Los Angeles Times,* April 27, 1993, business sec.

4. Kaufman, "Attention to Detail Spurs Stunning Turnaround."

5. Ibid.

6. Doler, "Informix's Phil White."

7. "CEO Lands on Top of the World," *San Francisco Business Times,* March 12, 1993.

8. John Eckhouse, "Stock Options Can Push Executive Pay into the Stratosphere," *San Francisco Chronicle,* May 10, 1993.

9. Nee, "Informix Is Back."

10. Kim Shanley, "History and Overview of the TPC," Transaction Processing Performance Council, http://www.tpc.org/information/about/history.asp.org (accessed June 14, 2004).

11. Nee, "Informix Is Back."

12. Sun Microsystems, "SPARCserver 1000 Running Informix Delivers Industry's Best Database Performance," news release, January 5, 1994.

13. Shanley, "History and Overview of the TPC."

14. Ibid.

15. Nee, "Informix Is Back."

16. Theresa Rigney, "The Sybase Enterprise," *DBMS Magazine,* May 1996.

17. Lafuente, "Popcorn, Popcorn, Popcorn."

18. Katherine Bull, "Nothing but Databases," *InformationWeek,* July 31, 1995.

19. "Oracle's Fatal Attraction," *Computerweekly,* December 8, 1994.

20. Clem Akins, "What Happen to the Oldies?" Google, September 22, 1997, http://groups.google.com/groups?q=informix+1991&start=60&hl=en&lr=&ie=UTF-8&selm=605lkr%24sf0%40cssun.mathcs.emory.edu&rnum=62 (accessed June 21, 2004).

21. T. C. Doyle, "Phillip White Gives Them Something to Talk About," *VARBusiness,* September 15, 1995.

22. Katherine Bull, "Power Play," *InformationWeek,* November 1994, http://www.informationweek.com/503/03iusyb.htm (accessed July 1, 2004).

23. Ibid.

24. Frank Hayes, "Sybase Keeps Powersoft Promise," *Computerworld,* November 6, 1995, http://www.computerworld.com/news/1995/story/0,11280,10808,00.html (accessed July 2, 2004).

25. Tom Henderson, "Database Dilemma," *Techweb,* September 1997, http://www.techweb.com/winmag/library/1997/0901/ntent006.htm?print=1 (accessed July 2, 2004).

## Chapter 4

1. Informix Software, Inc., 1995 Informix Annual Report (1995).
2. Amy Cortese, "Software: A Money Machine That's Firing on All Fronts," *BusinessWeek,* August 28, 1995.
3. Jim Collins, *Good to Great* (New York: Harper Business, 2001).
4. Doyle, "Phillip White Gives Them Something to Talk About."
5. Ibid.
6. Ibid.
7. Bull, "Nothing but Databases."
8. Doyle, "Phillip White Gives Them Something to Talk About."
9. Ibid.
10. Zahir Parpia, "Quote of the Week," University of Pittsburgh, January 1996, http://wwww.jamaica.ee.pitt.edu/Archives/NewsgroupArchives/comp.lsi/Jan1996/4009.txt (accessed September 7, 2004).
11. Doyle, "Phillip White Gives Them Something to Talk About."
12. Ibid.
13. Kim Nash, "Slow Sales Pull Sybase Down," *Computerworld,* April 17, 1995, http://www.highbeam.com/library/doc0.asp?docid=1P1:2851 3156 &refid=ink_pub_s4&skeyword=&teaser (accessed September 13, 2004).
14. "Sybase Inc.'s Stock Plunges by 41% on Profit Estimate," *Wall Street Journal,* April 5, 1995.
15. Katherine Bull, "System 11: Make or Break for Sybase," *Information-Week,* October 30, 1995, http://www.informationweek.com/551/51iusyb.htm (accessed September 20, 2004).
16. Ibid.
17. Ibid.
18. Ibid.
19. Ibid.
20. Nash, "Slow Sales Pull Sybase Down."
21. "Kertzman Speaks Candidly," *Sys-con Media,* September 1996, http://www.sys-con.com/pbdj/sep96/kertz.htm (accessed September 4, 2004).
22. Joan O'C. Hamilton, "Informix: Guerrilla Road Warrior," *Business-Week International Edition,* March 3, 1997.

23. Medora Lee, "Oracle Seeks a Truckload of Talent," thestreet.com, February 22, 1999, http://www.thestreet.com/pf/tech/software/718697 .html (accessed September 1, 2004).

24. Sun Microsystems, "Informix Enhances Superstores with Spectrum of Sun's Web-Based Enterprise Decision Support Systems," news release, April 8, 1997.

25. Bull, "Nothing but Databases."

26. Ibid.

27. Informix Software, Inc., 1995 Informix Annual Report (1995).

28. "Consolidations in the BI industry," *OLAP Report,* March 22, 2005, http://www.olapreport.com/consolidations.htm (accessed September 8, 2004).

## Chapter 5

1. David Carr, "Informix Ships Universal Server," *Web Week,* November 1996.

2. Julia Angwin, "Informix Beats Oracle to the Punch," *San Francisco Chronicle,* December 2, 1996.

3. John Davidson, "The Database Dithers," *Australian Financial Review,* April 12, 1996.

4. Rod Newing, "Database War Declared," *Financial Times,* October 2, 1996.

5. Kathleen O'Connor, "Clash of the Database Titans," *OReview,* March 1997.

6. Steve Ginsberg, "Can Informix 'DataBlades' Slay Oracle's Samurai CEO?" *San Francisco Business Times,* March 3, 1997, http://sanfrancisco .bizjournals.com/sanfrancisco/stories/1997/03/03/story3.html (accessed September 12, 2004).

7. Mike Ricciuti, "Informix Tries to Silence Oracle," *CNET News,* December 3, 1996, http://news.com.com/Informix+tries+to+silence+ Oracle/ 2100-1023_3-251624.html?tag=bplst (accessed September 15, 2004).

8. Steve Ginsburg, "Informix Aims Big-Gun Product at Rival Oracle," *San Francisco Business Times,* December 2, 1996, http://www.bizjournals .com/sanfrancisco/stories/1996/12/02/newscolumn3.html (accessed September 23, 2004).

9. Newing, "Database War Declared."

10. O'Connor, "Clash of the Database Titans."

11. Guy Mathews, "Informix Stands by Illustra Integration," *Computer Reseller News,* April 23, 1996, http://www.crn.vnunet.com/news/ 10164 (accessed September 12, 2004).

12. O'Connor, "Clash of the Database Titans."

13. Angwin, "Informix Beats Oracle to the Punch."

14. O'Connor, "Clash of the Database Titans."

15. Newing, "Database War Declared."

16. Ginsberg, "Can Informix 'DataBlades' Slay Oracle's Samurai CEO?"

17. Robert Ristelhueber, "Toxic Accounting," *Electronic Business Online,* March 1, 1998, http://www.reed-electronics.com/eb-mag/index.asp? layout=articlePrint&articleID=CA68050 (accessed September 16, 2004).

18. Ricciuti, "Informix Tries to Silence Oracle."

19. David Kalman, "A New Direction in DBMS: Montage Software's Dr. Michael R. Stonebraker Takes the Wraps Off His New Object-Relational DBMS," *DBMS Magazine,* February 1994.

20. Newing, "Database War Declared."

21. Bill Rosenblatt, "Informix Leaps to Objects," *Sunworld Online,* June 1996, http://sunsite.cs.msu.su/sunworldonline/swol-06-1996/swol-06 -cs.html (accessed September 9, 2004).

22. Kenny Maciver, "The Oracle Ecosystem," *Infoconomy,* September 6, 2001, http://www.infoconomy.com/pages/information-age/group 35588.adp (accessed September 12, 2004).

23. Martin Rennhackkamp, "Oracle7 Release 7.3," *DBMS Magazine,* November 1996, www.dbmsmag.com/9611d53.html (accessed September 18, 2004).

24. O'Connor, "Clash of the Database Titans."

25. John Foley, "Open the Gates to OBJECTS," *InformationWeek,* May 13, 1996.

26. Billy Wheeler, "Oracle/Sybase/Informix/MS-SQL," Google, December 23, 1996, http://groups.google.com/groups?q=oracle+sucks +1992&hl=en&lr=&ie=UTF-8&selm=59o4pp%241mp%40cssun .mathcs.emory.edu&rnum=2 (accessed September 12, 2004).

27. Brooke Crothers, "NT Catches Up to UNIX," *CNET News,* January 29, 1997, http://marketwatch-cnet.com.com/NT+catches+up+to+

UNIX/ 2100-1001_3-266101.html?tag=bplst (accessed September 12, 2004).

28. Ibid.
29. Rosenblatt, "Informix Leaps to Objects."
30. Mike Ricciuti, "Informix to Scuttle Flagship," *CNET News,* March 27, 1997, http://news.com.com/2100-1001_3-278336.html?part= msnbc-cnet (accessed September 15, 2004).
31. David, Kalman, "Informix and the Internet," *DBMS Magazine,* May 1996.
32. Bull, "Nothing but Databases."
33. "Informix Says Oracle 'Sleazy'," *CNET News,* January 28, 1997.
34. Douglas Harbrecht, "Oracle vs. Informix: The Battle of the Billboards," *BusinessWeek,* March 26, 1997, www.BusinessWeek.com/bwdaily/dnflash/march/new0326b.htm (accessed September 22, 2004).

## Chapter 6

1. Informix Software, Inc., 1997 Informix Annual Report (1997).
2. Ibid.
3. David Stodder, "Dialing for Hubris," *Database Programming and Design,* October 1997, http://www.dbpd.com/vault/9710edit.htm (accessed September 20, 2004).
4. Christine Macdonald, "Informix Reels from Loss," *CNET News,* May 1, 1997, http://news.com.com/2100-1001-279395.html?legacy=cnet &st.ne.fd.mdh (accessed September 24, 2004).
5. Lee Gomes, "Informix OKs $142m Shareholder Settlement," *Wall Street Journal Online,* ZDNET, May 26, 1999, http://news.zdnet.com/2100-9595_22514746.html?legacy=zdnn (accessed September 7, 2004).
6. Robert Lenzner and Emily Lambert, "Mr. Class Action," Forbes.com, February 16, 2004, http://www.keepmedia.com/pubs/Forbes/2004/02/16/363329?page=1 (accessed September 24, 2004).
7. Dow Jones, "Business Readings," Houghton Mifflin, May 1997, http://college.hmco.com/accounting/resources/students/readings/13-read.html (accessed September 28, 2004).
8. Ibid.

9. Geoffrey Moore, *Inside the Tornado* (New York: Harper Collins, 1996).
10. Informix Q3 1997 Financial Results and Restatement Teleconference, November 18, 1997, Menlo Park, California. All quoted passages from the teleconference are reproduced exactly as they appear in the written transcript.
11. Miranda Ewell, "Informix Settles Fraud Suit," *San Jose Mercury News,* May 27, 1999.
12. "Informix Corp: Settlement Official, Lawyers Take Their Shares," *Class Action Reporter,* http://bankrupt.com/CAR_Public/990528.MBX (accessed October 3, 2004).
13. Lee Gomes, "Informix Settles Holder Suits for $142 Million," *Wall Street Journal,* May 27, 1999.
14. "Informix Corp: Settlement Official, Lawyers Take Their Shares."
15. Stanford University Law School Securities Class-Action Clearinghouse, "Class Action Case No. C-98-0508-CRB," February 9, 1998, http://securities.stanford.edu/1009/COMS98/001.html (accessed September 1, 2004).
16. *Securities and Exchange Commission v. Phillip E. White,* United States District Court, Northern District of California, November 21, 2002, http://www.sec.gov/litigation/complaints/comp17855.htm (accessed May 4, 2004).
17. Informix Q3 1997 Financial Results and Restatement Teleconference.
18. Ibid.
19. Ibid.
20. Ibid.
21. Ristelhueber, "Toxic Accounting."
22. Informix Q3 1997 Financial Results and Restatement Teleconference.
23. *Securities and Exchange Commission v. Phillip E. White.*
24. Dow Jones, "Business Readings."
25. *Securities and Exchange Commission v. Phillip E. White.*
26. Dawn Kawamoto, "Options Called into Question," *CNET News,* July 28, 1998, http://news.com.com/2009-1001-213502.html?legacy=cnet (accessed September 20, 2004).
27. Informix Q3 1997 Financial Results and Restatement Teleconference.
28. Ibid.
29. Ibid.
30. Ibid.

31. Informix Software, Inc., 1997 Informix Annual Report (1997).

32. "Making It All Add Up," *CNET News,* May 12, 1997, http://news.com .com/2100-1001-279678.html?legacy=cnet&st.ne.fd.mdh (accessed September 1, 2004).

33. Wylie Wong, "Informix Chairman to Step Down as CEO," *CNET News,* May 6, 1999, http://news.com.com/2100-1001_3-225452 .html?part= msnbc-cnet (accessed October 2, 2004).

34. "Informix Settles Class-Action Suit," *CNNMONEY,* May 26, 1999, http://money.cnn.com/1999/05/26/technology/informix (accessed September 15, 2004).

35. Benny Evangelista, "Informix CEO to Step Down," *San Francisco Chronicle,* May 6, 1999.

36. Gavin McCormick, "IBM Buys Informix Division for $1 Billion," Boston Internet.com, April 24, 2001, http://Boston.Internet.com/ news/article.php/750851 (accessed September 20, 2004).

37. Ibid.

38. Ibid.

39. Wall Street Webcasting, "Chairman of Ascential Software Corporation States Being Very Well Positioned in a Very Important Market," June 11, 2002, *Wall Street Transcripts OnLine,* http://www.twst.com/notes/ articles/pam224.html (accessed September 2, 2004).

40. Stuart Lauchlan, "So Long Informix," *Computer Business Review,* January 5, 2001, http://www.cbronline.com/print_friendly/fae53472baa 40ad580256d350047ccde (accessed September 21, 2004).

41. Ibid.

42. Ristelhueber, "Toxic Accounting."

43. Ibid.

44. "Q&A with Oracle's Ray Lane, *VARbusiness,* March 2, 1998, http:// www.varbusiness.com/sections/98pages/lane.jhtml (accessed September 21, 2004).

## Chapter 7

1. Howard Mintz, "Informix's Infamy," *San Jose Mercury News,* June 28, 1999.

2. Howard Mintz, "Ex-Informix CEO Charged with Fraud: Accused of Concealing Scandal," *San Jose Mercury News,* November 22, 2002.

3. *Securities and Exchange Commission v. Phillip E. White.*
4. Securities and Exchange Commission, Litigation Release No. 18692, May 4, 2004, www.sec.gov/litigation/litreleases/lr18692.htm (accessed September 21, 2004).
5. Elliot Peters and John Keker, letter to Patrick Robbins, April 23, 2004.
6. Presentence Investigation Report (March 8, 2004), *United States v. Phillip E. White,* U.S. District Court, Northern District of California, San Francisco Division (No. CR-02-0375-CRB).
7. Mary Flood, "Fastow Lawyers' Weapons: Intensity and Intelligence," *Houston Chronicle,* October 4, 2002, http://www.chron.com/cs/CDA/story.hts/business/1601349 (accessed September 21, 2004).
8. Defendant Phillip E. White's Supplemental Sentencing Memorandum (May 26, 2004), *United States v. Phillip E. White,* U.S. District Court, Northern District of California, San Francisco Division (No. CR-02-0375-CRB).
9. Ibid.
10. United States' Sentencing Memorandum (May 12, 2004), *United States v. Phillip E. White,* U.S. District Court, Northern District of California, San Francisco Division (No. CR-02-0375-CRB).
11. Ibid.
12. Ibid.
13. Transcripts of Proceedings (May 14, 2004), *United States v. Phillip E. White,* U.S. District Court, Northern District of California, San Francisco Division (No. CR-02-0375-CRB).
14. Securities and Exchange Commission, Litigation Release No. 17016, May 21, 2001, http://www.sec.gov/litigation/litreleases/lr17016.htm (accessed September 23, 2004).
15. Presentence Investigation Report, *United States v. Phillip E. White.*
16. Ibid.
17. Reynolds Holding and William Carlsen, "Hollow Words," *San Francisco Chronicle,* November 16, 1999.
18. United States' Sentencing Memorandum, *United States v. Phillip E. White.*
19. Letter to Judge Breyer from Stephen Cutler (April 14, 2004), exhibit to United States' Sentencing Memorandum, *United States v. Phillip E. White.*

20. Ibid.
21. Peters and Keker, letter to Patrick Robbins.
22. Ibid.
23. United States' Sentencing Memorandum, *United States v. Phillip E. White.*
24. Ibid.
25. Presentence Investigation Report, *United States v. Phillip E. White.*

## Chapter 8

1. Robert Longley, "1 out of 32 Americans Under Correctional Supervision," September 3, 2003, About.com,usgovinfo.about.com/cs/censusstatistic/a/aainjail.htm?terms=american+women+prisoner (accessed September 12, 2004).
2. Bureau of Prisons, "Weekly Population Report," August 1, 2004, http://www.bop.gov/news/weekly_report.jsp (accessed August 4, 2004).
3. Phillip White, interview with the author, Atherton, California, July 24–27, 2004.

## Epilogue

1. Transcripts of Proceedings, *United States v. Philip E. White.*
2. David Shaw, "Why America Hates the Press," *Frontline,* http://www.pbs.org/wgbh/pages/frontline/shows/press/reactions/ (accessed October 1, 2004).

# Index

# About the Author

STEVE MARTIN BEGAN his career programming computers as a teenager in the late 1970s. For the following twenty years he worked for leading-edge Silicon Valley companies in roles ranging from salesperson to vice president. At Informix Software, Steve served in a variety of sales and sales management positions. He has also been a part of the executive teams at several high-technology start-ups. At Sqribe Technologies, he was a member of the leadership team that was responsible for driving revenues to $50 million over a two-year time frame. Sqribe Technologies was acquired at a valuation of over $300 million while in the process of its initial public offering.

Steve is the author of the critically acclaimed book about enterprise sales, *Heavy Hitter Selling: How Successful Salespeople Use Language and Intuition to Persuade Customers to Buy*. *Heavy Hitter Selling* is recommended reading by the Harvard Business School and has been featured in *Forbes* and the *Wall Street Journal*. The Heavy Hitter Selling concepts have been studied by leading companies around the world, including IBM, DuPont, and McAfee. The Heavy Hitter training program has helped thousands of salespeople master the customer relationship skills necessary to become Heavy Hitter revenue producers.

As a consultant, Steve helps high-tech companies develop and refine their business strategies, customer messaging, and sales operations. Specifically, he takes the customer's point of view in analyzing how to improve top-line revenue performance. As a result, the suggestive powers of a company's Web site, marketing collateral, and customer presentations are improved. The sales organization's operations and personnel are also aligned with market opportunities and competitive realities. Steve also works with executive teams to create a collaborative environment where engineering, sales, marketing, and administration work successfully as a team.

A highly sought-after speaker, Steve is both entertaining and provocative. He has made presentations to hundreds of companies and organizations, including Stanford University, the American Electronics Association, and the Norwest Venture Partners CEO Summit.

Visit www.storyofinformix.com for further consulting and keynote speaker information.

# Comments about *Heavy Hitter Selling*

"Like other sales books published recently, this one stresses the importance of human behavior. But unlike the others, it puts an emphasis on language. Salespeople could well benefit by exploring scientific models of language. Practical exercises make the book useful for everyone."—*Harvard Business School Review*

"Traditional selling focuses on product, price, and competition and misses the most important reason people buy--people and emotion. Heavy Hitter Selling offers a different perspective that is valuable in understanding how to win."—*Jay Fulcher, President and COO, Agile Software*

"I have experienced firsthand Steve Martin's success as a sales leader. It is rare to see someone translate his accomplishments into a well-written book with clear principles and a methodology that others can easily understand. It is a book you prefer your competitors not to have."—*Ofir Kedar, Founder and Past CEO, SQRIBE Technologies, Former Chairman, Brio Software*

"Recommended reading for the entire board of directors—especially venture capitalists who need to decipher and approve their portfolio companies' sales strategies."—*Dave Pidwell, Venture Partner, Alloy Ventures*

"Absolutely fascinating. A must-read for the management team of every company. Surviving today's challenging times may depend on it."—*Rich Heimsch, President, DEK International*

"I really enjoyed reading the book! An unusual way of looking at sales through perfecting the communications process. I agree, relationships and rapport lead to revenue."—*Dr. Shuki Bruck, Gordon Moore Professor of Computation and Neural Systems and Electrical Engineering, California Institute of Technology*

"This well-written, insightful book will give you ideas and strategies you can use to influence and persuade customers in any market."—*Brian Tracy, Author,* **Million Dollar Habits**